Living Through My Nightmare

Living Through My Nightmare

Levi Moore

All rights reserved. No part of this book may be reproduced, stored, or transmitted by any means, whether auditory, graphic, mechanical, or electronic without written permission of both publisher and author, except in the case of brief excerpts used in critical articles and reviews. Unauthorized reproduction of any part of this work is illegal and is punishable by law.

Copyright © 2022 Levi Moore

ISBN: 978-1-944662-80-6

Publishing date: September 2022

Cover Design by Othman Attaf

Dedication

This book is dedicated to Denise Halsey Moore,
Lucas Kenneth Moore, and Addison Clara Moore.

Contents

Dedication v

Chapter 1 Our Love/Our Loss 1

Chapter 2 Nightly Reflections 11

Chapter 3 Support Pieces 23

Chapter 4 Loneliness 31

Chapter 5 Staying Busy 41

Chapter 6 Exercise 47

Chapter 7 Work 59

Chapter 8 Holidays 73

Chapter 9 Therapy 81

Chapter 10 First Book 91

Chapter 11 Religion 101

Chapter 12 Medical Community 113

Chapter 13 Law 125

Chapter 14 Family 139

Chapter 15 Friends 149

Chapter 16 Coronavirus 167

Chapter 17 The House 175

Chapter 18 Being in Public 187

Chapter 19 Reflections of a Father 199

Chapter 20 Denise's Legacy 203

Chapter 21 Looking Back and Looking Forward 213

Acknowledgments 225

About the Author 227

Chapter 1

Our Love/Our Loss

Ten years ago, I met an incredible, compassionate, brilliant woman. Five years ago, I watched her and our full-term unborn twins die. I would say I lived an amazing five years with Denise and since then I've lived a nightmare. My time with Denise was filled with love and my time without her has been filled with pain and sorrow. No matter how bad the ending of her life was, the beginning of our life together was magical.

I first met Denise at work. She was a regular classroom teacher, and I taught special education. Once we started talking and she agreed to let me take her out to dinner and a movie, our life together quickly fell into a wonderful and joyous groove. We spent many weekends together, and I convinced Denise to drive with me from Raleigh, North Carolina, up to Ohio to surprise my father for his 60th birthday. I'll always remember driving right past my father, who was walking in the parking lot of the miniature castle where we stayed on that birthday visit.

That was the first time Denise met my parents and they very much liked her.

Denise really was a thoughtful person, and she was incredibly crafty. She put together a surprise 30th birthday for me and somehow convinced my parents to drive down from Ohio a month after we surprised them for my father's birthday. I never knew how she convinced my parents to come for the weekend, but they were there hidden away when I walked into Denise's apartment. Denise had even somehow reached out to a couple of my former co-workers when I taught in a different part of the state. She was amazingly generous and considerate. There were plenty of reasons I instantly took a liking to her, but it was the things she did for other people that made her who she was.

When Denise and I moved into our first home, it seemed right. We enjoyed our time shopping for furniture. Denise always had a knack for interior decorating, and our house showcased her abilities. We spent three and a half years in that house, the home where we shared love and happy times.

When Denise and I finally got married, we had already been living together, so in a practical sense it wasn't much of a change. However, our being married held a deeper meaning for us. Every time I looked down at the ring on my left hand, I felt like the most fortunate man to have this beautiful wife to come home to. The bond we shared made life so much better. It seemed our life was just beginning.

Despite our joy at being together, Denise held a profound desire to become a mother, but she continued to be disappointed that, unlike many of her friends and co-workers, she had not been able to conceive. We spent many tough months while she tried to get pregnant. I wanted to give Denise everything I could; sadly, some things were out of my control. I knew in my heart that if we could get pregnant, we would be set for the rest of our lives.

I didn't care if we could only have one child. We would have loved that child more than the world.

As we continued our attempts to become pregnant, Denise got the idea of upgrading our house. Its location wasn't ideal and the backyard was tiny. Sometimes, the best thing I could do as a husband was to let Denise be Denise, so I supported the decision to sell our house. Denise reached out to our friend who was a real estate agent, and after some time her friend was able to sell our house.

We decided to build a new home about the same size as our first one but in the back of our subdivision, where there would be less traffic and a much bigger yard. During the time between selling our first house and our new home's completion, we were able to spend time with her parents, who lived in the same subdivision and were only about a four-minute walk from both our old and new houses. Denise's parents were amazing hosts and extremely gracious to let us live with them for those few months.

One of the most exciting moments we experienced was the day we learned that Denise was finally pregnant. The whole family celebrated on that joyful day. During the period when we lived with Denise's parents, I took great pleasure in watching Denise and her mom talk about all things babies. They were both so excited!

I truly believe the day we received the news about our twins will go down as my best day in this life. I recall sitting in the doctor's exam room with Denise while she got an ultrasound, and they informed us we were going to have twins. I honestly can't think of a better day or better moment than when we heard this news. I couldn't stop smiling, and the look on Denise's face was beautiful.

Everything seemed to be coming together. We were going to move into a new house, start a family, and live close to her parents. I could see the next 50 years of my life unfolding on this amazing path with children and then grandchildren—all the years ahead with my wife, her family and ours, sharing unforgettable moments.

Once we moved into our house and bought our new furniture and cribs, that vision of the future seemed much more real. Finding out that we were going to have fraternal twins, a boy and a girl, made us even more excited. Denise and I had waited for several years to get where we were, and now everything seemed to be falling into place. We felt more than ready and deliriously happy to start this new adventure. We already had a lot of love in that house, and we were excited about sharing even more.

October 23, 2016, will forever be the single worst day of my life. As was generally the case during those days near the birth of our babies, I woke up excited and started getting all my weekend chores done so Denise and I could have the entire day to spend together. I went about my morning routine and waited to hear Denise stirring for the day. We were sleeping separately at the time because Denise slept so little that close to her delivery date.

When I finally walked into the master bedroom to see why she wasn't up, my life was shattered. A new life took its place, a terrible and tragic life, a life without Denise. Instantly, I knew something bad had happened. Denise had fallen out of bed and was leaning against her nightstand.

Shock is a strange thing. In that state of severe shock, I somehow managed to think clearly enough to phone 9-1-1. It took me a couple of tries to dial the numbers, but I was with it enough to go downstairs and unlock the front door before returning upstairs to be with Denise.

I was still giving her chest compressions when the first two emergency people showed up. They ushered me out and seemed to just look around the room. I wondered why they weren't doing anything, but I was still having such a hard time wrapping my brain around everything.

As more emergency personnel arrived, one of the older gentlemen sat me down and told me the news that forever changed the course of my life. He informed me that Denise had passed away. Instantly I asked about our full-term babies. He informed me that, with Denise deceased, the babies had passed away too.

There are no words for that moment—only tears and shock. As much as I didn't want to be the person on the receiving end of that news, I also would have hated to be the guy that had to give the news. Tragic and horrifying seemed too paltry to express the feeling.

When the investigator showed up, he said his name was Ryan. He was extremely gentle with me, as clearly I was completely unprepared for the devastation in which I found myself.

I told him I would be honest since the only thing I cared about was getting back into the room to be with Denise. Even though I was told she had passed away, I still longed to be by her side. Ryan let me know that my principal was outside as she heard the ambulance drive past her house (she lived in the same neighborhood). She received a text that no one ever wants to receive and was outside our home. I appreciated Ryan letting me know that, even in this ungodly world I was entering, there were still people who cared.

Ryan handled me with care and understood my need to get back into the room. We went through the questions and timeline, and, once he had enough information, he asked me to go outside where Denise's family had gathered. I had contacted them as soon as I could. I walked out of that house and into their arms. In all the world, there are never the right words to say under those circumstances.

After some time, the officers and medical personnel let me go back into the house to be with Denise. Sitting against the chest of drawers next to the body of the woman I loved, I poured my shattered heart out to her. Those moments are etched into my memory, and, though they were devastating beyond description, the only thing that would have been worse would be not being able to go in and talk to her.

Because of the nature of the tragedy, the police needed someone to stay in the room with me to make sure I didn't touch Denise's body or move anything before the people brought the stretcher and took her out of the house for the last time.

The man who came in to stay with me, whoever he was, had to be one of the strongest people I have ever encountered. I know he was crying, however, as he stood there watching me utter my sorrow and love to my bride, my best friend, and our unborn babies. How he must have felt to be the observer of such a moment. I don't know how he did it. Drowning in tears, I could barely do my part.

I spoke to Denise with the love that I had for her and the heartbreak of those babies passing. Those moments will be with me for the rest of my life, and I both ache to forget them yet never want to forget them.

At a certain point, the family headed back to Denise's parents' home, and my brother-in-law stayed with me as we watched the people from the coroner's office wheel in the empty stretcher and roll it out again, this time carrying Denise. As heartbroken as I felt in those moments, I still couldn't fully grasp how overwhelmed with sadness my life was going to be in the days, weeks, months, and years ahead.

The rest of the day was spent walking, looking at our photo albums, and letting people know what happened. When my parents arrived, I experienced another of those moments that I have no words to describe.

That night I barely slept. At one point, when I heard someone stirring halfway through the night, I got out of bed too. I ended up sobbing on the floor. I don't really think there is anything else that can be done during those dark moments.

The rest of the week was filled with family, planning the viewing and funeral, talking to people, and grieving. The viewing was long and therapeutic. Seeing all the people who cared was overwhelming. It meant a great deal to see how dearly loved Denise was by so many—people I've known for years, some I only recently met through Denise, and plenty of others I had never encountered. That night was tiring and beautiful. I was deeply moved by all who shared their love and admiration for Denise. As her body lay behind my right shoulder, no longer the vessel of her beloved, bright spirit, I listened to countless loved ones, friends, and acquaintances who honored her memory with their words.

When Denise's family, my parents, and I met with the funeral home, we weren't sure about what happened to the babies. The funeral home let us know they were removed and even took a picture of the babies before they were put in the casket at Denise's feet. No one could see them, and only people who asked knew they were there. The only image I ever got of those precious babies was from the funeral home's picture.

I still have a difficult time coming to grips with the fact that those two full-term twins never got to take their first breath in this world. They never had a chance to live or to see how beautiful the world can be. As much as I would have wanted to protect them from experiencing life's pain and heartache, I still would rather they had faced hardships than have this ending.

This earth was much darker that week, and, as much as I still had a huge amount of grieving and tears ahead of me, I don't think I will ever view the world as I saw it then. That will forever be the week that changed my life, and October 23rd will always be the day that changed who I was.

When events like this happen, someone in my position just wants the world to stop. I would have given anything for the entire planet to just stop and grieve someone who made others and the world better. Sadly, that wasn't the case. Denise passed about two weeks before a presidential election. The most intense, horrific devastation of my life occurred when much of the world talked only about the election. As a result, at the time I most needed to work through the intense grief, I felt cut off from those around me, whose focus remained on what now seemed far less important to me. Grief alters one's perspective profoundly.

A couple years after my soul-crushing loss, a tragedy occurred involving a school shooting in Texas—another one of those events where you just want to world to stop and mourn. In a horrible twist of fate, this happened at the same time as a highly publicized royal wedding in England. Early morning news anchors had the tough job of starting their broadcast talking about a horrible tragedy against the backdrop of a glamorous royal wedding. I remember watching how it all played out and grieving for those family members who surely must only have wanted the world to stop, and they didn't even get that.

In the last five years, I have changed in many beneficial ways but also in some unfortunate ones. I always say that I will never be a better person than I was the day I found Denise. I would make the argument that I may be more inspirational, but that doesn't mean better. My best day seems a lifetime ago, and I continue to deal with my grief and try to figure out how to endure and get through this new normal. I've dealt with thoughts of suicide and with seeing the world get darker even when it was unimaginable. I have seen things that brought me to tears, and I have found people who have been able to pick me up.

I'm not the person I was, but when tragedies on this level happen, I honestly don't think anyone could be the way they were before. There are aspects of me that I'm proud of, and there are parts I'm ashamed of. I don't think I would have it any other way.

In the past five years, I have figured out what I am made of and found a way to keep my head on mostly straight. I'm proud that I have made it this far, but I would give anything to have no idea what I'm made of and instead have the life I always wanted with a woman who brought out the best of me.

Denise was an incredible person; this tragedy won't change that. But her passing permanently altered me. When I look in the mirror, sometimes I see the person I used to be, but on other occasions I see a person I don't want to be. Either way, I will always know that I was a much better person with Denise in my life, and how our lives ended will forever leave a stain of devastation and loss on my soul. Instead of the life we dreamed of having, I live in a world I wish I had never known. I'm still here and I'm surviving. I've attempted to keep my head above water, and hopefully I've made Denise proud.

Chapter 2

Nightly Reflections

One of the things I miss most about my time with Denise is how much we communicated. I have always been a talker—much like my father. Almost as much as I enjoyed talking, I found great delight in listening. I used to come up with a random subjects for us to discuss. One of those was what we wanted to do when we died. I brought this subject up once when Denise and I were still in our old house. We both agreed that, after years of being together, we wanted to be cremated. I felt it was the best way to deal with our remains after we pass away. Denise also felt this was how we should handle our demise.

In a million years, I never expected *that* to be one of the most important life discussions we had. However, once Denise passed, I shared with the family that we actually had the conversation and this is what we both wanted, so after Denise and the babies passed away, we had them cremated together.

Denise and I could spend hours sharing our thoughts and delving into our ideas and dreams. She was such an intelligent person. The more I was around her, the smarter I felt, and I could tell the way I looked at life was much more worldly as a result of knowing her. I will forever miss the conversations we had. That first night, after I discovered Denise's body, I knew there were so many more words I wanted to say to her, but I would never get the chance.

Probably one of the best things I did after Denise died was to recognize that I still needed to talk to her and should continue to do that. Starting that first night, I wrote to her and I continued writing to her for over six months. I ended every day with her in mind. Doing this helped me to properly grieve this wonderful woman who was taken from all of us too soon.

After five years, I don't think I can truly tell you how devastated I was or accurately articulate how saddened and depressed I felt after she passed. I am not the man I was five years ago. The only thing I can do to reveal an inkling of how dark and sad the world was for me during those days is to share the words I wrote to Denise.

These are my "Nightly Reflections" that I wrote to her on a yellow legal pad for the first few days after she passed, when I was still shocked and shattered by the abrupt passing of my lovely wife and unborn babies.

10-23-16

Dear Sweetheart,

Today has been the worst day of my life. Today was the day I found you. I'm so sorry I didn't get to you sooner. For all my life, I will regret not checking on you sooner. I don't know what I am going to do without you. I'm still in shock, and I know I won't be getting any better. I really am at a loss for words, but I wanted to write to you to keep the memory of you alive. You were the very best part of me, and we had a lot of beautiful memories together. I am so sad I only knew you for a small amount of time but grateful that we filled the years we shared with such joy. I am really sad that I won't get to show you the Pandora charms I got for you. I know you are up in heaven with baby Lucas and our daughter (whatever name you have chosen for her). I told William that we were going to name our son after his family. I think that made him really proud.

This world is not as bright without you. You made me who I am today. I don't know why this happened, but I promise I will try to make you proud. Your mom was a wreck, and I think she is doing better, and I am holding up okay. I really don't know what to do, but I can't get the image of you out of my head. It will haunt me forever, and I just love you. I hope you take care of our twins. I want to meet them when I get to heaven. We will talk tomorrow. —Levi

Levi Moore

10-24-16

Dear Sweetheart,

Today I had a couple of breakdowns. You would have enjoyed my episode in the shower. I also had an episode last night, and I had a good cry. I really miss you and I hope you are up there with the twins. I really think you would be proud of how we are coming together as a family for you. Your mom is still struggling, and I can see her pain, and your dad is holding it together. Dawn [Denise's sister] has been very strong, and the four of us have really been keeping each other strong. I think we have an idea about a way to keep you remembered and to carry on your legacy.

For a bit, there were people here galore. We had about 10 people, and five of them were on the phone outside. You would have thought we were dealing drugs. I really miss you and shared a lot of thoughts with Derek today on a couple of walks. William and Anthony came over, and my friend Michael stopped by as well. We met with the detective, and he told us the best news. He told us you didn't suffer, that your death was quick, and you didn't feel any pain. I'm hoping between that thought and the Tylenol PM that maybe I will sleep better tonight. This world is still not better without you in it. Also, we will call the foundation the "Denise H. Moore Memorial Fund."

I love you so much and will love you forever. —Levi

10-25-16

Dear Sweetheart,

Today was an okay day. We met with the funeral home, and that was not as bad as I thought it was going to be. I have asked about trying to have an urn to keep your memories with me for the rest of my life. We are also looking at getting an urn for you and putting it in the thing at the church. I know you always wanted to take me to the church, and now you gave me a reason to do this. I also wanted you to know that Russ did us and you a big favor by setting up our fund, so it looks like we will be good for the Denise H. Moore Memorial Fund. I think this will be a really good thing for all of us.

We are also getting ready to talk about the service, and the pastor recommended that someone not so close try to get up there at the funeral, but I know I need to try. I am holding up okay knowing that I still get to see you two more times.

Your principal came over tonight with Mrs. Clark [my principal] and Mr. Baughan [my assistant principal]. I got to speak to your team, and they all were so sorry, but I think it helped in their healing process. Also, I am going to try to talk to my school tomorrow and attempt to get myself together for the big speech on Friday. I really want to make it the best it can be. Continue to know that I love you and will never forget the great times we shared. —Levi

Levi Moore

10-26-16

Dear Sweetheart,

I am one more day away from seeing you. We met with the preacher today to plan the memorial. I have started getting my speech together. It is not perfect but it is something I am proud of and something I think you will like. I also think that Amy is going to try to say something. Today she was fashionably late on two things. Also, the fund has been put out there, and Megan did a wonderful job with the "you care" page, and it sounds like Russ finished the other. I need to get the difference down between the two of them. However, I think you would be proud.

I am very excited to see you tomorrow. Dawn did a really good job over at your house. I told her about what happened. I think it helped her understand. Dawn and I have gotten very close, and we have worked as a great team. Brian [Dawn's husband] has been working on the film and not the PowerPoint presentation. I think you will be happy to know that we have a good amount of Jason Mraz on there. Do you remember when we went to see him in concert? Man, I was a great husband. I really miss you. I know I am doing well now, but the buildup to my big performance will be my crescendo. After that, I will fall off the cliff. Also, as you are up there, can you please look after your parents? They are really struggling. They aren't as busy as Dawn and I, so it is harder for them. Tomorrow I get to see you. I'm so excited to see you. I love you! —Levi

10-27-16

Dear Sweetheart,

Today has been a long day. I'm sure you saw how many people came out to pay their respects to you and to support us. Man, does my back hurt. I kept having to lean over and hug people. It is a good pain. I think you looked better after the viewing than you did earlier in the day. I know you absolutely hated the way you looked—with the pregnancy extra skin you had and the way you had to lie there. The funeral place did an excellent job of getting you together.

I really miss you, and I have been so busy, but after dropping dad off this evening, I got very lonely and I don't know how I will be next week. I think I'm going to be in an awful place after this all gets through. I can't believe that I will never get to hold our children. I am happy that you are with them and that you probably have a dog already. Olaf does love you. I was sitting here thinking of how much I am going to miss us watching *New Girl* and *How to Get Away with Murder*. I'm going to miss so much about you. We were so good together, and I am afraid the cliff is going to be bad for me. I also will be curious as to how I do tomorrow. I need to work on what I'm going to say a little more, and I need to get a line in there about how you were a pro at rolling your eyes. I will get one more time to see you tomorrow.
—Levi

Levi Moore

10-28-16

Dear Sweetheart,

    Today was a tough day. I was exhausted when I woke up and my stomach hurt. Good news is that I didn't pass out. The bad news is that today was the last day I would get to see you. It was hard but I know you would've been and were proud of me. I held it together very well. I was happy with my speech, and I think it was well received. I buckled when I walked in today.

    Also, you saw how well Jess, Amy, and Kelly did. Their speeches were very long; mine was not that long, and I really needed to pee. However, we made it through and your family did great. The balloon thing went pretty well. I wish I would have gotten a better picture but am happy nonetheless. When Brian and I went to Papa Murphy's, Jason Mraz was on the jukebox. It made me smile and then I got sad because it made me think of you. Man, I miss you. I miss you so much. This is going to be so hard. I even got sad that I remembered we still have a Disney trip we will never get to go on. There are so many things I'm going to miss and I see them everywhere. Everything is a constant reminder of the life we should have had. Everyone got to go back to their lives, and I have no idea what my life is now. I only know that I love you and that I will continue to write. I miss you so much. —Levi

10-29-16

Dear Sweetheart,

Today was the first day I didn't get to see you. It was hard. Everywhere I go, I see you or something reminds me of you. I am surrounded by so many memories we shared and haunted by thoughts of you and the reality of living in this world without you. I took a lot of stuff for granted—everything from food to getting help on my insurance.

I can't believe we are coming up on a week since your passing. I wish I could go back to a week ago and stay in the room with you. You were so beautiful before and during your pregnancy.

I was walking to the house earlier and saw a family sitting down for dinner. I felt sad and knew it was so unfair. That should have been us. I feel so empty without you and would really love to see you again. However, this is not realistic, and I know you are up in heaven with those kids of ours, and you are probably pretty upset at how bad the Cubs are playing.

One of my teeth has been hurting, and I think I might need to have it looked at. I know Dr. McConnell is going to be very sad about your passing. This all seems so unreal. I have a hole in my heart that will never be filled. I don't know how or if I will ever get over you. A large part of me doesn't want to get over you. I just want you to know that I love you and miss you so much. I made it through day #1 on the cliff. —Levi

Levi Moore

10-30-16

Dear Sweetheart,

    Today was a sad day. I'm starting to come to grips with the fact that you are no longer around. I am also beginning to realize that I took so much of the stuff you did for me for granted. Tomorrow I think I'm going to the park to celebrate the children's birthday. I know I need to do something. I also think I might try to go to Sunni Sky's, and I may even get you a sweet and salty ice cream.

    I miss you so much, and I notice myself changing quite a bit. I see big picture stuff now, and the little things don't really bother me much. I went to church today with Dawn, Brian, and Sara. It was good. Also, Dad and I were talking about the memorial fund after Bill asked us not to. Needless to say, my dad left soon after that.

    Your parents really miss you, and I know it is hard for them. I have filled my time with thinking of all the things I have to do. I think it's a good idea that I move back into our house tomorrow. Your parents need to grieve, and it will be hard for them with all the things Dad and I need to do. I think I am getting sick, which I don't care about since I'm not going back to school for a bit. I really have to try to figure out what I will do. Either way, that can wait since we have so much stuff to do. I love you and please watch over your parents. —Levi

10-31-16

Dear Sweetheart,

Today has had its ups and downs. Dad, Judy, Bill, and I went to Yates Mill Park to celebrate the kids. I hope you don't mind that we decided to call our daughter Addison. We wanted to have a name for her, and I really thought you were going to name her that. Anyway, I want to do something to remember them every year. We also went to Sunni Sky's. It was a good day. But I was really sad.

I love you with all of my heart and know that you are up in heaven, but it is not the same here without you. Your mom and dad and I went to your school. I talked with your assistant principal. She was very nice, but I had to chuckle because I thought about her secret.

A good thing that happened was Detective Ryan came over and sat with Dad and me while we passed out candy, which was a kind gesture. The guy who lives on the other side of the McKay's—I think his name is Chris—stopped over and talked politics, and it was not fun. I'm sure that you were smiling down on that one. Tomorrow, I think Dad and I will start making our rounds to try to figure everything out. I'm so thankful Dad is here as he has a lot of information that is good for me to think about. I just have a hard time believing you are not around. I don't even know if I can come to grips with it. I love you and miss you. —Levi

As I look over the words I wrote during those first few days, my mind is pulled back to lying in Denise's parents' spare bed that first night, putting the notepad on my leg and attempting to write and then trying to fall asleep.

Writing to Denise was the first successful idea I put in place as I grieved her loss. The reality of the situation is, although I didn't know it then, I understood truly how life-changing this event was and never felt ashamed of trying to put as many support pieces in place to better grieve Denise's catastrophic loss. The first night, writing to Denise, was a step in the right direction. However, thinking that writing to her would be enough to help me process and handle the grief would prove to be entirely wrong.

Writing to Denise helped me formulate a way forward so I could better cope with the new life I was going into—one without the woman who made me a better person. I'm forever grateful that I picked up that notepad. I so terribly missed all the discussions with Denise. Without writing to her that first night, I don't think I would have been able to deal with everything or put all the support pieces into place.

Chapter 3

Support Pieces

Writing to Denise every night for about six months helped me release some of the overwhelming grief onto the pages of my yellow notepad. When I occasionally looked back over my nightly entries, I could see some progress in how I was handling things over a span of time. During that time, I started to form ideas about what I needed to put in place to deal with the sad reality that was now my life. I still had a terrible uphill climb, but I could recognize, through my writings to her, that I was spending more time describing the day-to-day events and a little less on how I was struggling. Although the amount of sorrow still weighed heavily on me, gradually it was becoming less all-encompassing.

After about six months, I knew I needed to move on from my nightly reflections. I decided that while everything was still fresh in my mind, I would write down all my memories of Denise. I felt I needed to progress away from writing to her every night and also knew that, as time passed, I might lose some of those moments we shared if I didn't keep a record of them.

So I made a chronological list of everything we did and typed what I could remember for each of those events. This way I could continue to program my brain to remember all the good times we had and to not always dwell on how bad our ending was. This nightly exercise provided a way to reflect on how many joyful memories we shared in those brief five years we were together.

After I completed my chronicle of those five years, I was left wondering what to do next. I finally decided I would type the close to 200 nightly reflections I had handwritten to Denise. By doing so, I could continue to have the last thing I did before bed involve her. Going back over the first week of what I wrote to Denise, close to 10 months later, gave me an opportunity to see how far I'd come in a short amount of time. However, it also revealed that, although the rawness of those early days was gone, I was still in tremendous pain.

Even when I was on a vacation or visiting friends and trying to get out of that desperately lonely house, I always ended my nights with the thought of Denise. I ended up reviewing both the love story and the nightly reflections all the way to the end of the year. Over 14 months after Denise's passing, I still ended every night with the thought of Denise and an attempt to always remember her for who she was.

One of the other things I felt I needed to do was continue to look at pictures of Denise. A lot of people shy away from viewing photos of lost loved ones, but I really wanted to get to the point where I could see Denise's smile without being overwhelmed by sadness. For a couple years, that was really hard.

My brother and sister-in-law did a remarkable job of taking all of Denise's pictures to create the half-hour film that we showed during her viewing. A number of people watched the film multiple times as it was on repeat at her viewing. It was a beautiful film but was extremely tough to watch.

I still remember the week of Denise's passing, walking upstairs in my parents-in-law's house to see my brother-in-law with tears in his eyes trying to organize all the pictures and put the film to music. He did an incredible job. It was tough to watch the first time through, but I found seeing her beautiful face during the few seconds I had between visitors at the viewing somehow comforting.

I decided to attend church every week and visit Denise's final resting spot, then come home, and re-watch the video. Doing so proved to be absolutely overwhelming. I can't truly express how tough it was to watch that video every week. I would cry so much at the columbarium, the place where Denise and the babies' ashes and urn were located, and then return home to watch that video. I howled way more than I ever thought possible.

On the numerous occasions that my parents stayed with me, they couldn't bring themselves to watch it. Instead, they remained in the other room hearing me howl and cry. Even now, I pretty much have most of the film memorized and can feel the anxiety building as the pictures get to the first trimester picture of Denise at our first house. For whatever reason, that seems to be the one picture that affects me most.

Continuing to watch the film was really tough, but I knew the more I did so, the better I could handle all the pictures of Denise down the road. The goal was always to see Denise's picture and smile later in life and never to turn away from photos of her. I had to be incredibly strong to do that, and there were times I didn't think I could handle it, but I kept watching and re-watching every Sunday after going to church. I could hardly imagine that I had more tears after visiting her urn both before and after church, but I always seemed to have more tears. As difficult as that 30 minutes of video was for me, I hoped that in the long run the repeated viewings would pay off.

I watched this video weekly for nine months. At a certain time, I felt I needed to get away from these regular viewings and reserve the recording for birthdays and anniversaries. Only time would tell if I pushed myself too far into the grief and sadness.

As I continued to search for various forms of support in the year after Denise's passing, I read as much as I could to learn about how others overcame overwhelming grief. I found a number of well-written books that seemed to make me feel better and a few others that didn't seem to help. These books offered lots of ideas and insights (some definitely better than others). Ending the night with a book provided a helpful routine. After I wrote to Denise, I took my sleep medication and then skimmed a few chapters in an effort to cope with Denise's loss.

The idea of taking in as much content as I could about how others dealt with grief was probably more helpful than some of the books I read. I was able to hold onto the pieces from my reading that seemed to help. Sometimes, just being willing to try something is the best takeaway. If you can pick up one valuable insight, that makes the experience worth it. I am glad I continued to seek and discover different ideas, perspectives, and influences in my attempt to cope with this dark and ugly world I had entered after her passing.

Denise's parents and I attended a grief share class at the church we visited. It wasn't as beneficial as I hoped, but I was at least able to see other people in various stages of life and grief, which I found beneficial. Being around others who struggled with day-to-day living during such times of darkness was good for me. I was the youngest person there. I know I'm not supposed to compare my grief to that of others; however, my story was clearly one of the harder ones.

There was an older gentleman named David in the class. He and I were friendly; however, because they divided the class into small groups for discussion, we didn't get to spend much time with each other. The fact that we had lost our wives should have brought us closer, but the small group setup made it difficult for us to interact.

One day in church, after the completion of our grief share class, I was in the bathroom washing my hands when David walked in. He noticed my East Carolina University jacket and made a comment that his kids went to school there, but he was always a "Jayhawk."

I stared at him for a bit and asked, "You mean the Kansas Jayhawks?"

He said that indeed he was a fan of the Kansas Jayhawks. In a uniquely humorous moment, I started to untuck both my dress shirt and undershirt, and lifted my dress shirt to show him I was wearing a Kansas Jayhawks T-shirt. The detective who had investigated Denise's death lived in my neighborhood and had checked on me repeatedly as I mourned her loss. He had bought me this T-shirt as a present for me one Christmas.

David was delighted to see the T-shirt, and we quickly became much closer friends. We have since watched a couple of Kansas Jayhawks basketball games on TV, attended some minor league baseball games, and even shared various books about Kansas University. David and I needed something that would bring us together and, when we found it, we built a connection. I was grateful to have someone who could talk with me about our shared grief as well as run-of-the-mill sports. David is a wonderful and courteous person, one I would never have met if I hadn't put myself around others who were also in pain.

I encountered tough moments and feelings on a daily basis, but one thing that occupied a lot of my thinking was my wedding ring. It was a symbol of lost love. Many people who didn't know me thought I was happily married. They were both right and wrong. I had known the greatest happiness of my life while I was with Denise, and in my heart I was still married. But the woman I loved was gone, and that ring around my finger reminded me of those precious moments that were now gone.

In many of the books on grief, the length of time someone should keep their wedding ring on was discussed. As I processed my grief, I felt I might be able to remove it at the nine-month mark when I transitioned away from watching the film. However, when we got to that point, I realized I wasn't ready. I decided to try again on the one-year anniversary of her passing.

I don't think too many people have cried while waiting in line for the bank teller, but that day I did. I managed to carry my safety deposit box into the confidential room before my tears really started to flow. The removal of my ring for the last time was a reminder of how far I had fallen and how cruel the world could be.

I didn't want to take the ring off but knew at some point I had to and that there was a shelf-life of living with this symbol of my love with Denise. I was overwhelmed with emotion the entire day building up to that moment, but I kept moving as much as I could from the second my alarm went off that morning to the time I left work and drove to the bank. It was hard but I knew the only way to get where I needed to be was by taking the long, tough road.

I kept reminding myself that there were going to be a number of things that weren't going to be easy. The fact they were intensely difficult was strangely beneficial because it validated the depth and power of our love. The deeper the love, the harder the loss. As much as I wished my life could have been easier during that time, the level of pain I felt confirmed the truth of our love. When someone truly wonderful dies, things shouldn't go back to normal quickly. The more love you have, the more heartbroken you become when that person is ripped from your life. Looking back, I recall those moments of sobbing in a fetal position and understand that wasn't a bad thing. The loss of that level of love was bound to cause devastation. I didn't want it to be easier, but, man, was it often too hard.

I decided early on that I would lean into the grief, that I would face it head on, because I knew that was the only way I was ever going to get to where I needed to be and to a place that I, and Denise, would be proud. I never wanted to pretend that this tragedy wasn't as bad as it was. I knew the loss was on a level that I couldn't bear, and I never wanted to pretend it wasn't anything more than truly shattering.

I chose to never pretend I could function without properly addressing the severity of the loss. I leaned so far into the grief, my mind wondered if I was going to fly too close to the sun and burn up. This decision to lean in often resulted in me becoming too weak to deal with other aspects of life. But I never wanted to be one of those people who just *moved on* only to have the grief return at a later date. To me, putting all the support pieces in place and going full-steam ahead into the darkness was the only way to cope with the loss of Denise and our babies. I never wanted this kind of life, but I was played a god-awful hand, and the reality is, as much as I needed to lean on others, it was up to me to figure out how I could survive.

I will always love Denise. I somehow found the strength to face this mountain head on, but it broke me down and made me weak in the face of the obstacles that lay ahead.

Chapter 4
Loneliness

One of the biggest hurdles I have had to overcome is that of loneliness. It took a huge amount of time to be comfortable being by myself after everything happened. Only after about 2.5 years could I begin to do better with just being by myself.

In the beginning, I was really unprepared to go from loving my time at home with Denise to facing an empty house. By trying so hard to face this tragedy head on, I created a situation that was incredibly depressing and one I truly couldn't come to grips with.

I am an only child, and my parents live about eight hours away in Tennessee. I love my parents and their help in my time of crisis meant everything to me. When they came to stay with me pretty immediately after Denise's passing, they made me feel less alone. Coming home to their reassuring presence made a horrible time a little easier. My parents really supported me for that first six months. They needed to be with me, and I needed to have them there with me. Luckily, both of them were retired, so they had the time to spend with me. There were periods when they weren't able to be there, but I knew they would be back with me soon. Having them at the house when I arrived home helped keep my head above water. However, they couldn't be with me all the time, and I wouldn't have wanted them there every day. I knew I had to face my future as bleak as it was without a constant crutch.

Denise and I had moved to Raleigh to be close to her sister, and then, within a couple of months, her parents moved into our development. I felt like I truly never needed to form bonds outside of Denise and her family because I was so happy living Denise's life. I had my wife, and she was about all I needed. My dearest friend lived over an hour away, and those nearer to me in proximity weren't as close. However, when Denise passed away and I had to live by myself in our house, my loneliness progressed to a level that was almost unbearable.

Countless people stepped up to honor Denise and to help me, which I deeply appreciated. However, the idea of coming home after work every day to an empty house and waking up to do it all over again left me feeling lost and empty. I didn't really have a life of my own. Denise was pretty much my entire world, and without her I was truly alone.

One of the hardest challenges was that the intensity of the trauma of losing Denise and those babies left people with no idea how to talk to me or what to say. People often didn't ask me how I was doing and seemed afraid to talk to me about Denise, which left me feeling isolated and living inside my head a lot during those first couple of years.

I was just so unprepared for what happened. I lived with and *for* Denise. She was my everything. I didn't cultivate bonds outside my marriage, which left me in a vulnerable position when the worst came to pass. I clearly wasn't equipped to handle a world without Denise. I wanted to just fast-forward my life to a point where I was not so depressed and sad all the time.

When people did reach out to me, I found myself having to really watch my words. On multiple occasions, I said, "I don't want to live this life," and "my life should be with Denise." Both of those sentences expressed exactly how I felt, but they also sounded suicidal. Deep inside, I really didn't want to live without her. However, if I articulated that thought to someone, often they would think I was suicidal.

Although I really ached to have my world be different from what it was, I didn't want people to be afraid to talk to me for fear I would be pushed over the edge. I had to be careful about the way I shared my honest feelings. I also didn't want to make people feel uncomfortable. A couple of people in the neighborhood really looked after me. The investigator, Ryan, did a great job of trying to make me feel more comfortable in this world. I had never met him until I made that 9-1-1 call, and, all things considered, I was lucky he was on duty that day. I am thankful to him for sharing these thoughts for the book.

From Ryan Blackwell, Former Investigator

> *I still remember sitting in my chair in the living room and getting the call on that Sunday morning. I was informed that I needed to go to a house that was so close I could probably walk there. I still recall all the baby things out, the chili that was in the crockpot, and the blueberry pastries that were out for breakfast. I remember talking to Levi upstairs in the bonus room; it was such a tough scene.*

When I got home later, it felt really weird and I was pretty exhausted even though it was still early in the morning. I had family coming over that afternoon, and I had to be happy and upbeat and put on a happy face while the family was here, and that was difficult.

About the next day, I checked in on how everything was progressing with Denise's autopsy. I knew she had been well deceased for a while by the time Levi got there because I could clearly see Rigor mortis had already sat in. I think I was able to come talk to the family almost the next day to tell them that she died quickly.

I did really enjoy picking up some pizza and coming over and hanging out with Levi and his dad on Halloween. It seemed to help Levi that someone else was there and around. I remember walking with him and Levi telling me as we walked around the neighborhood how uncomfortable it was knowing families sitting down at dinner knowing that Levi just lost his family.

I believe that when Levi dies he will be reunited with Denise. When he sees Denise, he will want to tell her all about what has happened in his life since she died. I know that Denise will turn to Levi and let him know that he doesn't need to say a word, that she has been watching him ever since. Denise sees everything that Levi is doing and has done.

Another person who supported me in my time of grief was my neighbor Adam, who lived next door. Because Denise and I were only in the house for a short time, Denise never got to meet Adam or his family. In a weird way, it was almost easier for people who didn't know Denise to talk with me. Those who knew her had their own grief to process and also had a deeper realization of how sad this loss was. I could be honest with Adam and Ryan about how I was truly feeling. I had the ability to talk with them about how dark things were, and they were still strong enough to deal with my pain.

Before Denise died, I actually was a fun, upbeat person most of the time. I take after my father in that way. My dad is probably the most genuine and happy person anyone has ever met. I don't think I had really seen my father sad more than once before this situation arrived at our front door. I've seen the way my father acts and lives, and, for the life of me, I want to be like that. For a long time, I was. But after Denise's death, I just tried to avoid bringing a whole lot of sadness into people's lives. I never wanted to drop darkness into someone's world, but there were those who could identify that, as much as I didn't want to do that, it was exactly what I *needed* to do.

As much as I struggle to talk to others about what I was going through, I had a difficult time relating to other people as well. I used to look at Facebook just to see what my acquaintances were doing. I enjoyed the pictures of places other people had been, and it was a wonderful way to keep track of the lives of those I didn't see on a daily basis or to connect with one of my good friends and ask about something they posted to start a conversation.

After I lost Denise and the babies, I really struggled with looking at Facebook. I was so weak in those moments that I really had a difficult time being happy for others. I felt angry with myself for being jealous of their joyful lives. I hated the idea that so many people had wonderful lives while I had to take medication just to fall asleep. I selfishly wanted the world to stop and address my needs, but that doesn't happen in this world. As I watched the lives of others moving on, I tried so hard to be pleased for them, but my own version of life was so miserable that I couldn't muster such feelings. I spent my evenings trying to watch a movie when all I wanted was to get a phone call from someone to just say, "Tell me how you are doing and don't pretty it up."

Being inside that house in the state of mind I was in felt overwhelming. I didn't want this to be my life. My only hope was that I could survive long enough that, maybe, I wouldn't be a true shell of the man anymore.

Over time, I got better at reading my moods and tried to put healthy things into my life. I finally got smart with my phone. It represented my ability to talk and to be reached. But spending too much time on it drained me. After I removed Facebook, I decided I would check my normal evening apps (local and national news, sports information, and movie information) and then put my phone in the other room. Since I rarely used my computer to do anything other than financial work and download podcasts, I was effectively removing myself from social media.

I know it sounds like such a small thing, but this change made a huge difference. Just the fact that I was no longer looking at my phone and focusing on other people's happy lives while I lived in whatever depressing world I was living in helped my head settle. I did better at trying to enjoy television rather than checking my phone every couple of minutes in hopes of hearing from people I desperately wished would reach out to me.

I realize I could have made the effort to connect to people, but it was simply too difficult. What would I even say? I would ask how they were and wait for them to politely respond with the same question, knowing they might not want to hear the answer. I didn't want to be that guy who always dumps his sadness on others.

I used to always ask myself, "How could this be worse?" Sometimes asking yourself that question can put a horrible situation into perspective. The reality was things could always be worse. My situation was unbearable, but frankly it could have been so much worse. We could have had those babies in the hospital, experienced the ultimate joy of that moment, and then had some terrible accident that ended up with the same result of Denise and our children dying. If I were the driver in that scenario, being the person responsible for their demise rather than a witness, I doubt I could ever have recovered. As bad as the situation was, I reminded myself that there are always worse occurrences.

One night, I spoke with a friend who used to be in the military, and he brought up a subject I had thought about a number of times. He told me that some of his military veterans had gotten emotional support dogs to help with the transition back into non-combat zones. I really feel a dog would have helped me by being a true companion at the house during those lonely nights. I am not sure how I would have managed taking care of a dog while I was at school, but, if I would have been up to the responsibilities, I think a loving dog would have given me some comfort. I just didn't think I could handle taking care of another life when I could barely keep my head above water.

Another area that caused discomfort was my desire for compassion rather than pity. I always believed that pity was short-lived and counterproductive while compassion provided long-term, honest support. I longed for compassion but wanted nothing to do with pity or people who acted out of guilt or obligation.

Denise and I experienced an issue with a neighbor while in our first home. I go to bed early, and it takes me a long time to fall asleep. One December, our neighbor was playing loud Christmas music after 9:30 p.m. (four hours past sundown). I walked over and asked them to please turn it off so I could sleep, and they did—no harm, no foul.

A couple of days later, I was in the kitchen, and Denise made a noise and looked at me. I asked what was up. She stared at her phone and said, "Nothing." Clearly it wasn't "nothing," so I asked what it was. She asked me to promise not to get mad, and I said I couldn't do that but that I wanted to know. She told me the neighbors who had played the loud music had made a snarky comment on our neighborhood Facebook site about my asking them to turn it off. Denise didn't want me to confront them about the remark, but, seeing as how I teach my students not to use social media to bully and say things they wouldn't normally say, I put on my shoes and headed to the neighbors' house.

I told them both—much more politely than many people might have—that I was two doors down if they ever wanted to say something like that, so they could come tell me to my face. They acted apologetic, but I knew they were just being defensive. Needless to say, they didn't like me after that.

After Denise died and the entire neighborhood knew, I was out one day walking with a friend. I always just wave or hold my hand up to acknowledge anyone in the neighborhood. I passed that husband on my walk and spontaneously raised my hand in acknowledgment. He just stared at me without returning the gesture.

I was so bloody proud of that man. I am sure he knew what happened, but he didn't show me pity or false encouragement. I told the guy with me how proud of that man I was because that neighbor, who clearly didn't like me, wasn't being fake to me. He didn't *pretend* to care. Even though some people might have held that lack of response or compassion against him, I was thankful he hadn't feigned an emotion he didn't feel. He didn't show me the pity that so many other people had. He was true and honest. Although he wasn't *nice*, he was everything I needed him to be at that time.

As I continued to deal with the loneliness, I was fortunate to stay as busy as I could. As a child, I struggled a lot with my attention deficit hyperactivity disorder (ADHD), but, after Denise's passing, this disorder actually made it much easier for me to stay active and to find as many outlets as possible to keep treading water and remain afloat. Being busy with various projects kept me from focusing solely on the nightmarish turn my life had taken. I longed to fast-forward to a time when things were better. However, for so long I really wrestled with those countless hours alone in that house we had shared. All I could do was to keep moving, trying to accomplish some kind of forward motion.

Chapter 5

Staying Busy

Early on during my darkness, I couldn't seem to rest. I no longer had the ability to just sit and relax or watch a movie. I struggled with my anxiousness and what to do with myself because of how mad at the world I was. During a trip to a mall, I came across a LEGO Architecture set. I had put together a few of these while watching football with Denise and enjoyed them. I decided to buy one and see if that would occupy my restless mind.

Sure enough, once I started, these construction projects captured my focus, and I spent a lot of money buying as many as I could in order to put them together each night. I figured this was a much better way of handling the aftermath of a devastating tragedy than grabbing a bottle of alcohol or pills. During those first four months, I spent so much of my non-work time just building these sets. I found it therapeutic to start a project, work through the process, and see how it turned out. I put all my completed projects upstairs in the loft overlooking the entryway. However, as time went on, I got to a point where I could spend more time on the couch relaxing.

My neighbor Adam, who was such a kind friend, was gracious enough to buy me a big LEGO set and a bunch of DVDs. They helped me to while away all the hours before my nightly ritual of writing to Denise, taking my sleep meds, and reading before falling asleep. The medication helped me to drift off, but, if I woke up during the night, it was nearly impossible to fall back to sleep. Instead, I lay there trying to shut off my brain and let go of the pent-up anger and anxiety.

After several months, I could move more away from the LEGO projects, but I still suffered from so much anxiety that, in order to cope, I needed to remain busy. Watching *The Big Bang Theory* DVDs that Adam bought me helped a great deal with my ability to relax, but I still needed and wanted to stay occupied as much as I could.

When I was in college, one of my assignments was to draw a dream house. What I designed was really just a gym with a place to sleep above it. After that memory popped into my mind one day, I created a plan for my dream house and then tried to make that out of LEGO bricks. Although I wasn't constructing the sets anymore, I still needed to keep my brain occupied and felt that making my own structure would challenge me. I ordered each piece to build the base and started drawing on graph paper. I set up one floor at a time, drew my ideas, and then figured out what color each piece would be and how many different bricks and colors I would need for that story. It was a large amount of work, but it kept my mind engaged. I placed a big LEGO order, which then arrived a couple weeks later and then tried to assemble each level, complete with the pieces that represented furniture, koi ponds, gym accessories, stairs, and walls. It took me about half a year to finally finish the structure, building multiple stories on top of each other. It was quite impressive by the time I completed it and helped me maintain focus on something other than my misery.

As I worked on the project, I got the idea to create something as a thank you for those who had helped me through my grief. I drew, designed, and ordered pieces in order to build a model of my neighbor Adam's house on a much smaller scale. We always joked about how creepy it was that I was taking pictures of the outside of his house and pretending like I wasn't paying attention to what the inside of his house looked like. This smaller project allowed me to continue to navigate my grief while also showing a wonderful neighbor how much I appreciated all he was doing for me.

Adam even found a Kansas Jayhawks basketball arena that was made by a different building set company. He bought it for me, and I took it over to my parents and put it together one Christmas. This great gift planted a seed in my head of other things I could do to thank those who continued to reach out to me. I made Adam the University of North Carolina basketball arena, built the University of Connecticut basketball stadium for my friends the Cawleys, and constructed the University of Alabama football stadium, the most challenging one of all, for my friends the Huffmans. Making things for others helped me to focus on something other than myself and my grief and allowed me a way to repay those whose kindness meant the world to me. I think everyone enjoyed the models I made for them and appreciated the time I took to put them together.

Listening to podcasts was another means of focusing my attention. I always had my earbuds in. I started downloading podcasts before I knew Denise and found them a great way to learn. While I was with her, I listened to them while exercising or during my morning routines. After she died, there was rarely a moment when I wasn't listening to podcasts—when I exercised, while I did housework or made my lunch, even while pausing a movie to go to the bathroom. I welcomed the distraction from the misery of my existence. Finding content that interested me related to sports, movies, and news was never an issue. Hearing someone's voice through my earbuds alleviated the loneliness of the house. Often, the worst part of my day was my time in the shower when I couldn't be distracted by people talking and was just left to my own thoughts.

Cleaning the house wasn't always fun, but that, too, occupied my hours spent at home alone. As much as I hated mowing the lawn, it kept my attention engaged as well. These tasks weren't absorbing, but they had to be done and could be grounding.

I have always been a list maker. I assigned myself one chore to complete every day after school, which meant there were fewer to accomplish during my weekends. I always bought groceries on Friday and went to Target or to get gas on my way home on weeknights. I tried to just check things off my list to feel some sort of accomplishment. I maintained a list of weekend chores that included washing the sheets, towels, or clothes, keeping up with the finances, cutting my hair, and preparing my lunches for the week. I still found relaxing difficult, even though I needed to rest my body. As time went on, I gradually became less anxious, but the list of tasks around the house remained.

Much of my life became just finding ways to while away the night. I had no idea what to do with myself. Going from a happy home with the love of your life to a place of silence devastates the psyche and breaks the heart. I tried to cope with the loss by structuring my life around routines included teaching, errands, chores, and pastimes that required my focus. Then, hopefully, I could make it to about 8:00 p.m. when I would begin my ritual of writing, reading, medicating, and falling asleep.

Eventually, I found myself able to relax in front of the TV during the weekends. I had always enjoyed sports before Denise's passing. Initially, I couldn't bring myself to care much about any of it; however, as time progressed, I took some comfort in watching sports and movies. My dad urged me to get out and go to the movies because that was something I could do by myself without feeling uncomfortable. I tried that a couple of times, but I came home tired and even got headaches during the movies. It just wasn't the best use of my time.

Between the loneliness and the ability to find constructive ways to deal with loss and this new semblance of a life, I struggled just to survive. I was fortunate to find avenues that helped, but there was no playbook for what I was dealing with. I continued to stay active both inside and outside of the house. Luckily, I always enjoyed exercising and recognized it as an outlet for me to both feel good about myself and keep from drowning in sorrow. The projects I completed gave me a way to pass the time and feel some kind of satisfaction. I understood the need to stay engaged and busy both inside and outside of the house as I continued to navigate this world of loss.

Chapter 6

Exercise

During college, one evening when my roommates were being annoying, I went running and slept much better than usual. After that, I started doing some exercise every night as a way to wind down, and it also seemed to improve my mood. I felt better about myself. Later, also in college, I began to go to the gym early in the morning to lift weights. As time progressed, I pretty much kept up that routine. Exercising allowed me to be outside and to meet people and also to feel comfortable. I took some pride in sticking to my regular exercise routine and felt I was a much more balanced person after some form of physical activity.

After Denise passed, I felt totally adrift and had a difficult time forming thoughts and articulating my feelings. Walks with my dad or my friend Derek seemed to anchor me somewhat and provide some semblance of stability. Because I had such a difficult time eating that first week, I ingested mostly milkshakes and smoothies. After the first week passed and the second week turned into trying to take care of all the logistics and financial ramifications of losing Denise, I started going to the gym every morning. I wasn't back at work yet and wasn't sleeping through the night despite the medication. Thankfully, I could sleep in as late as I needed to, eat my banana, and then head out the door to the gym. Before I went to the fitness center and after I came home, my life was still a tragedy. I needed to release the overwhelming pent-up energy somehow, and I felt at least mildly better after some physical exertion.

After I started back to work, I would go to the gym as many mornings as I could. There were still a number of days I had some meetings and didn't have the time to drive there.

One of Denise's cousins started a campaign to support me, and, with the generous contributions of many of her friends, I received way more money than I expected—enough to purchase an elliptical machine for the house. I felt such gratitude for the generous donations and believe I put their well wishes to good use.

On those days when I couldn't make it to the gym, I could just hop on the elliptical and do a workout, which slightly reduced my stress level. At that point, even a modest reduction was still a huge deal. In the dark place where I was, the difference between functional and not functioning was a miniscule amount. The elliptical helped bridge the minor difference on those days, especially those crushing Sundays when I went to church and sat by Denise's urn. On those days, I cried so much that I needed to drink a large amount of water just to avoid headaches. Since the gym wasn't open before church on Sunday's, I grabbed my Gatorade, put on my shoes, and hopped on the elliptical for a half hour. While it didn't solve all my problems, this exercise routine helped me immensely to release some of the emotional energy.

As I continued to progress and as time went on, I tried to get away from watching Denise's film every Sunday after church. However, I didn't know how to fill the time I had allotted to viewing it. One day, standing in church, watching all the people who were happy and rejoicing as I fought back tears, I had the thought that I should spend that time in the gym, which I did from the nine-month mark on every Sunday after church.

At the time, I was essentially exercising in some form pretty much every day. For years, I had gone on a long run on Saturday mornings. After Denise passed away, I pretty much quit running for a bit. It wore me out too much, and I didn't enjoy it. As a result, I had this block of time every Saturday morning where I felt guilty if I didn't do something. I ended up going to our neighborhood pool to swim as many laps as I could.

I've never been a superb swimmer and have struggled with the amount of water I intake while trying to breathe properly. But with practice, as I swam slowly back and forth in the pool, I became decent at it. On those Saturday mornings at the pool, I met a couple of older retirees who were always really fun to talk to after I finished my laps. I made a point of arriving early to get my lane before all the kids started coming because I didn't want to be the cranky guy who told them to stay out of my part of the swimming pool.

Swimming provided a welcome respite from my mental anguish, and I could still shower and get home in time for my tutoring session with one of my former students. As summer waned and the cooler days of autumn approached, I left the pool behind and opted for a longer workout at the gym. Those workouts helped me process much of my feelings and frustrations.

I continued my walks in the neighborhood, sometimes with neighbors or people who were kind enough to come over and take a stroll with me. The neighborhood had a couple of walking paths and several places where I could just be outside. Over time, though, I felt drawn to get back to running.

I had run marathons in the past, so the idea of struggling to run two miles was new to me. I had to start small. I liked the idea that I could just put my shoes on, go outside my house, and run a couple of miles. Not having to drive anywhere was a relief.

While it was slow going at first, over time I built my legs and cardio up to the point of trying a couple of 5K races. One of my co-workers, Eileen, who was always a good friend, mentioned trying to do a 5K together at some point. I was strongly in favor of this idea.

I still had no idea how to talk to strangers, so being around people who knew my situation helped. With those who didn't know me, I was always two questions away from dropping sadness onto an unsuspecting individual.

Eileen and I found a race for a good charity and enjoyed taking part in it. After we got our breath back, we discussed trying to do more. We decided to research races in the Raleigh area for charities we wanted to support. That summer we ran about five different races, one a month. It felt good to contribute.

Another one of our co-workers, Lindsay, joined us on July 4th for a race that supported individuals who were trying to get back on their feet. Having something like a 5K to train for and look forward to and staying active in the process helped me tremendously. I don't know if Eileen will ever fully understand how much those little races helped me make it through that really tough summer.

As much as I enjoyed the monthly races, my head was still all over the place when I wasn't focused on something, so I continued the structure of running on Saturday mornings, even when there were no races. I felt so much better after I ran five or six miles that I continued to keep it up. I could get up, go for my run, shower, and then tutor on Saturday mornings. After that, I ate lunch and then often take a nap. That way I had spent half the day with activities that drew my mind out of the abyss and allowed me to feel a little more myself.

I've spent a lot of time considering the many aspects of my grief-stricken life. So many things changed in me after that fateful day. One of them was that I developed a distrust of doctors and the medical community in general. We will discuss more about this in later chapters, but I think part of the reason I tried to maintain my health through exercise was that I no longer wanted to rely on doctors. Of course, I loved exercising before this tragedy, and after Denise's passing I found workouts provided great relief from my constant distress, but, if we wanted to psychoanalyze this part of me, I would agree there is an argument to be had that I also wanted to stay fit enough not to need medical help.

Exercising helped to settle my head and keep me moving forward, even though the amount of frustration and anger I held was often way too difficult to manage. The fact was that exercising seemed to have an incredibly positive impact on my mental health. I'm fortunate that I enjoyed physical activity as much as I did and hope I can continue to use it as a stress reliever and means of coping until I climb fully out of this place of despair.

Apart from my own coping methods, I needed to be around people. Being active and running races provided some social contact, which eased my feelings of loneliness and gave me a sense of belonging. About two years after Denise passed away, my friend and co-worker Lindsay got the idea of putting together a relay race team.

I had participated in and enjoyed relay races in the past and was delighted she had invited me. We were trying to get 12 people to run from Raleigh, North Carolina, to the beach. The race would start early Friday morning, and 200 miles later we would arrive at the beach. I was enthusiastic about the running part but even more excited about just being around people. Our team consisted of fellow teachers, parents, and some friends. I asked my good friend and speed demon William Lucas to join our team, and he agreed. I didn't realize until the day before the event that William and I would be the only men on the team. I wasn't sure how everything would go, but I knew most people and figured it would be a good time.

We split our team into two vans. The first vehicle, which was organized by Lindsay, was a large 15-passenger van. The second, a mini-van, carried seven people including me. I can honestly say that trip was the greatest 1.5 days I have ever spent in a mini-van. Our team was cracking jokes, discussing how much slower we were as runners than the people in the other van, and overall just having a blast. I honestly don't know when the last time was that I laughed so hard. I was amazed that we were all still laughing at 3:00 a.m. Those events are only as good as the people you are around. The six other people in our van were William, Eileen, our amazing co-worker and loyal friend, Jeannie, Jeannie's sister, who was our chauffer, and a couple of others. We had such an incredible time. It was one of the most fun experiences I had ever been involved in.

I enjoyed encountering new people and being around other runners at exchange zones, where one team's runner would pass to someone on another team. We laughed, joked, and slept outside an elementary school. It was great. I was especially pleased to meet my friend Meredith for the first time there.

My van of runners was about ready to start the seventh leg, which would have been the first time we ran, and our other team members were cheering for our runner, someone named Meredith whom I had never met. She sprinted really quickly and handed off to our fastest runner. I looked down at Meredith's leg and noticed it was bleeding. I asked if she was all right and, in the most beautiful Southern drawl, she replied, "I think I fell." It was a priceless moment.

After the race, we all agreed it was a wonderful time and went back to our homes. I was exhausted after the event. But more than that, going from such an enjoyable couple of days back to my sad life brought a painful sense of contrast. At the time, I felt grateful for the lift in spirits the event offered. It gave me a good amount of hope.

I continued running on weekends by myself until at one point my friend Lindsay asked if I would be interested in running with her and Meredith one weekend. I always felt awkward around new people because I still had no idea what to say when they asked about my life. Luckily, Lindsay understood that and I knew she would make things much more manageable. I had such a good time running and trying to keep up with Meredith and Lindsay that they agreed to let me run with them more often.

Those runs every Saturday were probably the best thing I had going for me outside of work. Both of them were pleasant company, and, after a couple of trips, Meredith clearly knew of my situation, so I could just talk openly about things. Both Meredith and Lindsay were kind and caring. The biggest problem became how much slower I was than they were, so I tried hard to keep up with them as much as I could. Over time, Lindsay became such an impressive athlete that even Meredith couldn't keep up with her.

When Lindsay moved to the other side of town, she wasn't able to run with us as often, and she was also doing much more intense workouts than I could do. I kept running with Meredith, and even now, every Saturday morning, Meredith and I run and talk. We discuss pretty much anything and everything. We chat about our ups and downs, how work is going, how all the dating stuff is going (or not going), and the two of us have become very close. I still find Meredith's kindness to me remarkable. Most people found it difficult to have open discussions with me. Meredith was one of the few people who realized that, yes, it's challenging to talk about the kinds of issues I'm still dealing with, but the worst thing you can do to a person in my situation is to *not* talk to them.

A friend once told me he was having a hard time but felt he couldn't come to me with his problems because they didn't even begin to compare to what I was facing. It's hard to complain about how your kids are keeping you up at night and you struggle to get sleep to a guy that literally watched his wife and unborn twins die. He was right about it being a challenge; I understand that. However, if you don't talk to me, then you are further isolating me and putting me out on an island alone. I need to converse with people. The best support someone can give me is to treat me like a person and a friend. If I'm not able to deal with it, that's on me. But I need to have interactions with people if I'm ever going to be able to function in a social environment.

Being around our relay team and then getting to run with Meredith and Lindsay was such a welcome relief because I was around people who cared. I know it must be hard to be around someone in my situation, but avoiding me is way worse. I need people that are healthy for me to be around. I don't honestly know if I could have picked a better friend to spend an insane amount of miles, smiles, and races with than Meredith. She is a true gem. She didn't know me before my life became a wreck, but she treated me as a friend would, and that is exactly what she is, a great friend.

From Meredith Poole, Friend and Running Partner

The Tuna Run is my favorite weekend of the year. I connected with Lindsay at a gym in Raleigh in the fall of 2018. We had mutual friends during our time at Appalachian State University and were both going to the same morning workout classes. Lindsay invited me to run one morning and told me she had an opening for the Tuna Run Relay that October. I was immediately interested. She told me about the people who were on the 12-person team and promised it would be a good time. I had just accepted a permanent job in the Raleigh area and thought this would be a great way to make friends.

I ran with Lindsay and a few girls from our van before the relay on weekday mornings. We talked about how excited we were, how we would deal with the sleep deprivation, and they also filled me in about who was on the team and how everyone was connected. I knew a lot of the relay team was connected through Lindsay's school. They told me specifically about one of the guys on the team, Levi. They explained his situation and my heart immediately broke for this guy.

The Tuna Run is a total of 36 legs to total approximately 200 miles from Garner (North Carolina) to Atlantic Beach (North Carolina). Most people divide the 12-person team into two vans, which connect every six legs at an exchange zone. I met Levi at the first exchange zone. He was bubbly, cracking corny jokes (nothing has changed since then), and overall the van clown. His fellow team members were already describing some of the bizarre college stories Levi was telling. I was amazed at how well Levi was intermingling with the group despite the awful tragedy he had endured. I was introduced to Levi and he welcomed me to the team.

Our group saw the other van at two more exchange zones before the final leg at the boardwalk at Atlantic Beach. At one of the exchange zones, I ran in with a bloody knee after falling during my 3.1-mile night run. I got a little too close to the white line and tripped. Of course, another van saw the incident, but I was too embarrassed to acknowledge them. I just popped up off the road and yelled, "I'm good!" and kept trucking to the exchange zone. As I ran into the exchange zone, the teacher mode came out of my teammates, and they immediately cleaned me up and put Band-Aids on the scrapes on my knees and elbows. We met the other van and they were all asking what happened to me or who pushed me down. The team still likes to tease me about the fall and claims that, when I ran in, I exclaimed, "I think I fell!"

The Tuna Run wrapped up at Atlantic Beach around lunchtime that Saturday. Our team enjoyed the seared tuna, BBQ, and drinks the relay provided us. We went over the funny stories that happened in each van and talked about the good, the bad, and the ugly of the relay. It was unspoken but we all agreed we would be back the next year.

The next goal for Lindsay and me after the relay was the Wrightsville Beach Marathon. We spent Tuesday, Thursday, and Saturday mornings training together. Our Saturday mornings were dedicated to our long runs. Lindsay invited Levi to join us for part of an 18-miler in Holly Springs one Saturday morning. I was still amazed how Levi was able to assimilate to any group. He was talkative, humble, and friendly. He went over the physical and mental challenges of the marathon distance since the Wrightsville Marathon would be our first. I enjoyed running with Levi. Later we would realize he was not exaggerating about the challenge.

After the marathon, Lindsay and I would run with Levi sometimes on Saturdays. Due to conflicting calendars, sometimes Levi and I would be the only ones running. I worried at first it would be awkward or we would run out of things to talk about, but it was the complete opposite. We would finish our 10 miles and still have topics to discuss. Lindsay moved, so Saturday mornings eventually became just Levi and me running. We would meet at a park in Raleigh and run anywhere from six to 14 miles. Saturday mornings became my favorite time of the week; it was my therapy. Levi and I discussed everything from the week: work and personal challenges, the highs and lows of the week, and what the weekend before us held. I once told him that I felt like the problems I complained about paled in comparison to what he had endured. He reassured me that he would much rather me tell him about my struggles because he appreciated people just treating him like a normal person instead of focusing on the event.

Levi and I trained for the Oak Island Marathon. Our mileage went up tremendously to a few long runs of 22 miles. We still did not run out of topics to discuss. We continued to run after the marathon just for fun. It's been almost two years since the marathon, and we still meet most Saturdays to run. I am appreciative for all the miles Levi has listened to me, provided advice, and shared his corny jokes.

Chapter 7
Work

As bad as my life was and often still is, there is one constant that helps me rest my head on my pillow at night: my students. I absolutely love teaching my students. They are not perfectly behaved all the time, but they are kids, and I love the idea that my job is to build a rapport with them, understand them, and teach them as much as I can in the allotted time I spend with them each day.

As I special education teacher, I get to work with kids over multiple years and watch them grow. With these students, I have found my place and my joy. I work with many of the fourth and fifth graders and love the students at that age. I also enjoy speaking with their parents about their children's journey while they are still in elementary school and how we hope to transition them smoothly into middle school.

I am always in a good frame of mind when I can just focus on my kids. I went into teaching to focus on the kids. With all the other responsibilities that come with my work, it can be challenging at times to concentrate on the kids. But, in those moments when those kids are my sole point of attention, and we are working hard and having a good time learning, there are few jobs better.

The elementary school where I work and very much the principal probably single-handedly saved my life. I have always enjoyed teaching. I'm definitely not the best teacher out there, but when the world got bad, my kids were always there for me. The first year I taught at my present school, I had the chance to work with a group of first graders. I followed those students all the way to fifth grade. When Denise passed away, the best medicine for me was to be in my classroom teaching those students. It wasn't easy, of course. I spent hours in a co-workers' offices pouring out my emotions in an attempt to release the darkness from my mind so that, when the bell rang, I could give my students the best I had. I will be forever grateful to those students and their wonderful parents who gave me some form of calm in a world that made little to no sense to me.

My principal, who lived in my neighborhood, who got the worst text message ever, and who was outside when one of her employees was being interviewed by the police because his wife and unborn twins had just passed away, treated me the way I needed to be treated. I can't imagine there were any administrative classes that she took that ever dealt with what I was bringing to her table and to her school. I think some of the best leaders are the ones who can take off their professional hats and put on their personal hats, and that is what my principal did. I will be forever grateful that she did everything she could to help me transition back into the job so I could get away from that empty house, and all that darkness, for 40 hours a week.

Living through my Nightmare

From Danielle Clark, Principal

It was a typical Sunday morning on October 23, 2016, at the Clark residence. My husband and I were preparing for the owner of Garden Hut to come to our house to provide some landscaping ideas. My little boy, Ryan, who was three at the time, was keeping me busy in the loft. All of a sudden, my husband and I heard sirens blazing through our quiet neighborhood. I remember saying, "What could be happening?" My husband, who was previously in the Navy and Fire Service, shared with me that emergency personnel didn't make those kinds of interruptions unless something was wrong. My husband jumped in his car to see if he could find where the sirens were coming from. He texted me to let me know the police and ambulances were at Levi's house. Levi Moore and his wife Denise lived in my neighborhood. She was pregnant with twins, and all of a sudden I just had this uneasy feeling. I became the principal of a school that Levi worked at in 2015. I just wanted to check on him and know that all was okay, so I texted him. I received a text on my phone with the words, "She's gone. The babies are gone too." Immediately, I started shaking and had the chills. I told my husband, "I have to go." He asked if I wanted to have him drive me, so we all ended up in the car.

When I arrived at the house, I was able to talk to a nice neighbor, tears streaming down my face. I knew that I was hurting, but I had to be strong. I couldn't believe that my friend and staff member was suffering this inconceivable loss. School was tomorrow and there was no way Levi would be there. His wife was also a teacher, and the principal of her school and I were friends as we started our principalship at the same time. I told my husband to go, and I just stood outside the house, praying and thinking millions of things going through my mind. As I walked up the street, I called a mentor principal, asking for the Crisis Response line for the district. When I finished talking to the district office, I also cried with the principal where Levi's wife worked at the time. Now, I had to put my principal hat on. I called my area superintendent and met the other principal, her social worker, and her school psychologist at Denise's school. In addition, I notified my school counselor and school psychologist. My school psychologist's husband was the counselor at the school in which Levi's wife worked. There were many connections already between my school and hers. We spent several hours consoling each other and working with district personnel on this devastating matter. On that Sunday afternoon, October 23, 2016, at 3:16 p.m., I wrote an email to my staff that I will never forget, sharing the news about Levi's situation and calling a staff meeting at 8:00 a.m. the next morning. The other school did the same thing.

For days, I checked on Levi, texting back and forth. We would speak on the phone. He would cry, and I would cry, just grieving for him. As a principal, all I could think about was supporting him from afar and supporting my current staff with whom he had formed so many relationships. I put together a

Google link allowing all staff the opportunity to attend the viewing on Friday, October 28, 2016. All of the surrounding Southern area schools supported the two schools. The outpouring of support was just incredible and lasted for several weeks until Levi returned to his safe haven, school. Without his school family, his own family, and his students, Levi said many times, he would have struggled to do life differently.

Writing this today, several years later, I would want anyone reading this to know that this tragedy has never been forgotten. During the month of October every year since I have been principal, I check on Levi. It was difficult then, and it is still difficult for the people who experience trauma. The phrase that sticks in my mind is support your people. Build relationships and get to know everyone on a personal level because people matter! People are who get us through difficult times.

As much as I thank my principal, it's only right that I express my gratitude to my fellow co-workers. After Denise passed and I returned to work, my co-workers stepped up and for the remainder of those two months until winter break; they took care of all of my meetings and most of my paperwork. I still completed my report cards during quiet moments when I couldn't deal with the world. My teammates helped me deal with the transition into the school as much as my principal did. Without all of them, I don't think I would have been able to get back to work, and I really doubt that I would have made it this far.

The idea that teaching special education is and always will be about the kids is wishful thinking. I went into this field believing that only the kids mattered. However, as documentation, lawyers, and disagreements over money continued to grow, so did the amount of paperwork of special education teachers. About 90% of my time when I'm not teaching is spent on paperwork, setting up and conducting meetings, sending emails, etc. The hardest part of my job is dealing with parents in a conference room instead of devoting my attention to students in a class. As education continues to transform, we all expend more and more time dealing with the conference room rather than the classroom.

This has always been a frustration and one that often makes me question how long I can be a teacher. At what point do I decide to just become a teaching assistant who does much the same job for significantly reduced pay? When will I put my money where my mouth is and only focus on the kids as a teaching assistant? Who knows when that will happen, but teaching kids is all I really care about. Handling the paperwork continues to be a thorn in my side, but it's the job that I have to do in order to pay the bills.

The job of being a special education teacher is one that consists of being extremely organized and being able to stay on top of all the paperwork. This was much easier to do when I went home to a lovely wife and a beautiful life. Without Denise and the comfort of our life together, I found it incredibly difficult to keep functioning the way I had before this tragedy. Without my principal and the other special education teachers who took much of my paperwork those first two months, I very well might not be alive today.

As much as I love and still love teaching, I could see and feel myself changing at work. I realized I was no longer the same person after this tragedy happened, but I didn't know how I would handle the aspects of my job that could be frustrating. The paperwork was part of the issue, but there were other situations that I wasn't able to handle as I had before.

Restraining a child because he was a danger to himself or others became a lot more challenging for me. Having lost my own children, dealing with those who were out of control in my classroom was truly difficult. I remember trying to help with a student in the office who was having a difficult time and who had slapped a school employee. I could feel the difference inside myself between how I dealt with such issues before and after Denise's passing. I think the other staff members saw it in my eyes, and, once things calmed down, they let me get back to my classroom and collect myself. The person I used to be was much calmer and more centered in the face of such chaos.

Caring parents always make my job so much better, and I must say I have had the great fortune of working with an amazing number of truly terrific parents at my school. This hasn't always been the case, but I feel gratified that I get the chance to work with wonderful families. On the flip side, the parents who try my patience clearly have a much more pronounced effect on me since Denise passed. When I try to talk to parents during carpool duties at the end of the day and ask to meet with them, and they blow me off, those moments sting much worse now. Those incidents eat away at me, especially coming at the close of the school day. I would prefer that such exchanges happened earlier in the day because there would be more activity and class to help me forget about those interactions by the time I went home.

One of the responsibilities I have during the first couple of weeks of the school year is to help visitors. Often these include the parents of the new kindergarteners. I can still remember standing there, welcoming all this smiling parents and little kindergarten kids. Outwardly, I tried to be composed and friendly while inside all I could think was that I would never get to walk little Lucas and Addison into school the way those parents were. I felt sad and frustrated and, yes, even jealous. Envy was the hardest emotion I had to face. I needed to come to terms with the fact that there were going to be many events, happy times, and special moments that I probably will never have. It's a sad reality. But it's the jealousy that I will have to deal with. Seeing all those parents walk those kids in every year was tough. The year isn't far off when I should have been the one holding the hands of my little ones on their first day of school. The thought of it was heartbreaking.

Traumatic events have an effect on people no matter what their profession, but when it comes to losing a child, teaching is high on the list of jobs that could trigger someone in my shoes. Even though I never got to meet them, I loved Addison and Lucas. The idea of teaching other people's children when I never got to share such moments with my own may seem impossible. But it's the work I've known and the path that fulfills me, and I'm grateful to have those kids in my classes who enrich my life in so many ways. I'm proud that I manage to continue in the profession despite the devastating loss.

In fact, I did well enough at work that over time it became a negative in my life outside work. As the situation with Denise's family continued to evolve, I was pretty lonely. Work was really the main constant in my life, and, as long as I was teaching, it *looked* like I was doing well. Many of the people at work saw how buoyed I was in the classroom with the students, who lifted my spirits, and probably thought I was doing much better than I actually was. What they didn't see was that I really had no constant outside of my job, that I went home to an empty house and a relentless grief. I am sure there were people who saw me being upbeat, feeding off my kids' hard work, and thought I was well enough that they didn't need to reach out and check on me.

That was the side effect of having one really good thing in my life. But the reality was those moments in the classroom were the polar opposite to the hours alone inside my house.

I nurtured such good relationships with my kids, and fortunately I had plenty of them. I remember the first full school year after Denise passed; I had a fifth-grade student with autism whom I had worked with for years. This girl and I had a great rapport. In previous years, there were times when I was teaching that I could hear her howling in another classroom because she had gotten upset. She was so loud we could hear her four classrooms down. I used to tell the students in my class, "Keep doing what you're doing; I'll be right back." As I strode down the hall, many of the other teachers were looking around or shutting their doors. I went into this girl's class, took her by the wrist, and, still wailing and howling, she walked with me down the hallway. When we got back to my room, she would fall down, and I'd shut the door. I would look at her and say, "You've got one minute!" Then I'd turn to the other students and say, "She has one minute." As she continued to howl, she always looked over her shoulder at me. I just looked at her. Slowly, after about 30 seconds, there was more breathing than wailing, and finally after the minute she became quiet. I loved that girl so much, and we became wonderful friends.

When she was in fifth grade, I was still teaching her, and I will always remember how she stayed with me for an additional 15 minutes after I walked the other kids back to their classroom. We would laugh and joke on the way back to the classroom trailer where I taught that year. When we got back to the class, I would put a pretty difficult fraction problem on the board and then just sit back and watch.

This girl would draw her lines and circles and do all the things I had taught her for adding and subtracting fractions with unlike denominators, and she would solve the problem. I constantly told myself that, yeah, my life sucks, but I've got *this* and I'm good at this. Just watching her solve this type of problem that, honestly, based on her limitations and her behavioral issues, she probably shouldn't have been able to solve, soothed my senses. I knew that the biggest reason she was able to solve those problems correctly had little to do with my academic skills; it was because I was really good at building a relationship with that girl. We had such a great rapport that I could teach her to solve problems that were often way harder than anyone could have predicted just a couple of years earlier.

It's not about being a great academic. I'm gifted at encouraging my students and believing in them so much that they want to work and please me. I'm less of a teacher and more of a motivator. There are few teachers who are actually great at both the curriculum and the relationship side, but there are a number of those outstanding teachers at my school, and they are some of the finest people who don't make nearly the money they deserve.

During those really tough couple of years, I leaned into those relationships that I had built with many of my kids. I was given the opportunity to tutor one of my former students, and we kept that up for a couple of years. She was one of the fifth graders whom I taught during the year of Denise's passing, and her compassionate and wonderful family was really there for me. I am forever thankful that I got to meet them.

I also had the good fortune to catch up with a former parent during one of the 5K races I did with Eileen and some other friends. When this mom and I spoke, she mentioned her son had loved his time working with me. Ben was always such a great kid. My only complaint was that when I started to get onto him for laughing and not focusing on his work, he just grinned at me. I would finally say, "Ben, you're in trouble; stop smiling." At that point, we just couldn't help laughing. I got to catch up with him a couple of times. Ben is now bigger than me, and, although I managed to win one game with him, he is much better at basketball than I am.

Since seeing his mom at the 5K, Ben and I have gotten together on a number of occasions and watched soccer matches, laughed a lot, and he even set up a dinner at Panera with a fellow student, and we all hung out there for about four hours. Leaning into these relationships allowed me to be social in my comfort zone with a former student and also just to spend time with good people.

For a couple of years prior to Denise's passing, our school had an after-school running program. Although I never participated in them while Denise was alive, I did attend their 5k events and even got beaten by a couple of little kids.

After Denise passed, I joined in on these types of after-school activities and programs. I now help with both the running program and the soccer program that my friend Lindsay started. I felt like I could just be me at these kinds of social situations. Since I didn't feel comfortable in most other settings, those after-school athletic events provided an important outlet for me, even if they were tiring after working eight hours.

I truly believe that the school, my fellow teachers and staff, and those wonderful parents and kids probably saved my life. I always wondered if I would have been able to survive if I had worked in a cubicle or some corporate office. I think the answer is no. My time with my students was probably one of the biggest factors in my survival. When I was with those kids, they didn't see me as a grieving man, which gave me a chance to step out of my misery. I definitely wasn't 100 percent even with them, but being able to focus on my students helped tremendously with my ability to keep my head above water.

During the third year after Denise passed, I helped with a presentation. I had attended an excellent technology conference in downtown Raleigh for a couple of years. The conference offered many technology sessions. There was one special education session I felt especially drawn to and knew I needed to attend, but I was disappointed that the presenters didn't show up. I always thought it was weird that no one knew or told us the session wasn't going to happen. As a result, about 12 other people and I sat around waiting. After it was clear the presentation was unlikely to happen, one woman stood up and asked if we wanted to talk about things we use in our classrooms that benefit the kids. We all agreed and she started sharing. A couple of other people chimed in, and then I started throwing out ideas about how we could use these ideas when we talk with parents. We all got something out of the session. Afterward, I went to introduce myself to the woman who had first spoken, and she said her name was Kira. As we were talking, someone came up and said we did a great job and that we should think of presenting the next year.

I've never been a spotlight-on-me kind of guy, but what we did was far better than having a no-show presenter, so we discussed the idea and indeed the following year we presented. We got the Friday at 8:30 a.m. time slot and faced an audience that was far larger than I wanted or imagined. Almost all the people who were attending from my school showed up early to support us. Our presentation about the technology tool for special education seemed to be well received. I don't have too many gifts, but one of my true talents is identifying amazing people and attempting to ride their coattails. That's essentially what I did. Kira was incredible. I did a good job of flowing through our PowerPoint slides and adding comments and suggestions; however, Kira was so far above me when it came to leadership, and she did such a great job. It was really great watching Kira work the room and be an amazing leader.

To most individuals, doing a presentation like that would be no big deal. Many people do them regularly. I am not one of those people. I keep my head down and try my hardest to focus on my kids. I'll always be proud of the fact that, even in those terrible years, I was able to put myself out there and present before a large audience with someone from a different school whom I didn't really know well. I identified it as a step in the right direction. Although I was shaking in my car while driving to the conference that morning, I'm glad I could put myself in such an uncomfortable situation and accomplish the task.

School and teaching brought Denise and me together, and I take great pride in the fact that I can still show up to school and work and try to do right by my students. As much as I'm proud of the job I do, I will always remember something my father-in-law told me after Denise passed away. He looked at me a couple weeks after her death and said, "Think of all those kids who won't get Denise as their teacher." It was probably one of the most profound statements I've ever heard. While I'm really proud I can still go to school and teach those kids, I'm also deeply saddened that so many kids who could have had Denise as a teacher never got the chance. As much as I enjoy and like teaching, I don't think I will ever be half the teacher Denise was, and that is probably one of the toughest pills I have to swallow.

Chapter 8
Holidays

The holidays that Denise and I shared were wonderful. Most consisted of spending time with her loving family. Denise was always a great host when we would have people over to the house, and we spent many of our holidays at either her parent's or her sister's home. We cherished those times together.

Denise loved the Christmas season above all other holidays and took great pride in decorating the tree. I learned early on that my place during this annual ritual was on the couch, but when that special time came, I got to open the boxes of ornaments and hand them to her while she figured out where everything went. I was pretty good at my totally emasculating role.

Regardless, seeing Denise's eyes gleam with joy was all I ever wanted for Christmas anyway. Even so, I was delighted the year she gave me the gift of a book of dates. My last present was a box containing 12 envelopes, each representing something that we would do together each month the following year. It was essentially a gift of monthly experiences. Some were sweet and others were more humorous. My favorite was the evening she allowed me to set up the tent in our loft, and we watched the movie *Goonies* and then slept in the tent. They were all really fun experiences. When Denise was alive, all my holidays were much brighter.

After Denise passed, clearly my anticipation of the holidays was significantly different. It took a great deal of time, years in fact, for me to handle those times I once cherished. Even though the holidays aren't as challenging now after the passage of time, they pale compared to the days of joy when she was here. I've managed to go from what were truly devastating experiences in the first couple of years after her passing to passable holidays, which is more of a reflection on past sadness than it is on current happiness.

It will be no surprise when I tell you that first Christmas was the worst of my life. I had lost Denise and our twins two months prior, and the buildup to the holiday season was devastating. I saw all these commercials and heard people talk about what they were going to do and how excited they were, and I could barely even make it to Christmas. I was in such bad mental shape and didn't know how I would handle it.

Denise's family and I decided it would be good to go on a cruise. Getting out of the house that Christmas afternoon was really smart. Instead of sitting in the place of our beautiful memories in a state close to the abyss, I found some measure of happiness by spending time with her family and my niece Sara, who was my roommate on the voyage.

The holiday season is wonderful for those who are joyful, but it can break you down and tear you apart if you're not happy. That first Christmas morning, I watched Sara open her presents and went to visit Denise at the columbarium before going home.

The closest I have ever come to actually wanting to die and commit suicide was that Christmas morning in the shower.

While I was at our house, I still wore my earbuds and constantly listened to podcasts, but in the shower I was left to my own devices. The day after Denise died, I collapsed into a fetal position, sobbing as the water poured over me. The sorrow I felt seemed to devour me until I was an empty shell. Two months later, standing in the shower, I was struck with the knowing that no Christmas would ever be the same. Helpless and alone, that was the single closest moment to taking my life I ever experienced.

As I stood there, the thought crossed my mind that suicide rates go up during the holiday season, and I just realized why. It was a good thing on that day that I didn't own any guns. I was never really worried about injuring others, but I was concerned about harming myself. If there was ever a day I would have felt comfortable taking my life, it was that first Christmas without Denise.

I have spent most of my major holidays talking to Denise at the niche that holds Denise and the babies' urn. That first Christmas, I bought Denise some presents and a card. Trying to keep Denise's memory alive mattered a great deal to me. I wrote a note in the card and took it to the columbarium and read it to her. That practice became my new normal for the holidays. I know it's a weird tradition, but I feel it is still ours. I will be the first person to admit that trying to find a card to read to a deceased spouse isn't easy. I'm not the target audience for most of the card makers, but I've managed to find a number of cards that get to the heart of the message I want to impart, cards that are fitting for someone who was loved as dearly as I loved Denise.

I spent every Valentine's Day, Mother's Day, wedding anniversary, Denise's birthday, and most Christmases at the niche. As time went on, I spent a couple of Christmases with my family in Tennessee. However, before I left, I always made it a point to visit Denise's niche at the church and go to her school to sit on the bench dedicated to her. I don't really think there was any other way I should have spent those sad holidays than with the person I loved, reading those cards and the words I wrote to her. I still have all those cards that hold the words from my heart to the woman I loved.

The first couple of years, I spent many of those holidays with Denise's family. It was good to be together during those days of deep grief. But at a certain point, as the family dynamics evolved and I continued to change, I didn't attend as regularly as I had immediately after Denise's passing.

Those first couple of years were hard on all of us. The reality was that I went home to an empty house while Denise's parents and sister didn't. Every day, they had other family members to hold and support them, to share the burden of their pain. I was all alone. I ached to have someone to confide in, to share the moments of misery.

At a certain point in the grief journey, I found it was better for my mental health if I wasn't around them on the holidays. I knew Denise's family missed her every day, but so did I, and we were only together as a full group on the holidays. I was in such a terrible depression every day that it became challenging for me to only be around them on those few holiday occasions and then return to my sad life. For those precious moments, I felt like part of the group, but then a day later, people returned to their lives, and I was left alone in my torment. It was easier after a while not to connect for such a short period because it increased the feelings of loneliness and sorrow afterward.

The contrast of those moments of togetherness and support against the backdrop of every other unimaginably lonely, tormented day became too much to bear.

The trauma of losing Denise was shattering and filled me with a lot of anger. One of the worst aspects of the emotional upheaval was navigating feelings of jealousy because others had what I had lost, which in turn brought on guilt over even entertaining such emotions. No one wants to be the person whose friend loses a spouse, but most would almost certainly agree that it's not as difficult as being the one whose life partner dies. Having nothing for so long really messed with my emotions.

For the first couple of years, her family and I released balloons to honor her and the babies. Those were the days when I continued to watch the film commemorating her life. Seeing Denise's smile and how much life she had made it impossible to not feel terrible and pathetic. Only after enough time had passed was I able to better handle those photographs. When I watch the video after five years, I still feel the incredible sadness, but the gnawing pain and rawness are gone. As difficult as it was at the time, I was smart to program myself to the point of being able to see Denise's smile in those photos and feel some measure of grace.

In those first years, small things affected me greatly while I lived alone with my ever-present grief during the holiday season. Getting Christmas cards in those first three years was torture. Finding my mailbox filled with cards depicting happy families sent me into an overwhelming pit of anger and sadness. No one wants to admit that they hate seeing photos of happy families, but, boy, those moments were hard. The cards that actually helped to ease the pain were those from people who knew how badly I was doing, who reached out to check on me. Those cards meant that someone was trying to include me and to let me know they cared.

But the cards from people who had no idea how to talk to me and didn't care to try, well, those broke my heart. Smiling faces on family photos that revealed how well their lives were going left me devastated. I never told them so, of course. I could decide not to look at social media sites, but I couldn't avoid my mail. I had a stack of cards from people who obviously sent them to make themselves feel better. I made sure to place someone who made me smile on the top of the pile. I still remember a good friend in Ohio named Roger sent me a couple cards that I always loved to see. He was about eight hours away, and I hadn't seen him in close to 15 years, yet he reached out to show he cared.

It would be wrong and inappropriate to get angry at people over such things. The world went on despite my grief, and, as much as I hated the Christmas cards, at least I was still alive to look at them. Total isolation would be the mistaken way to handle my life, so I continued to stretch myself to face challenges in the hope it would help me later.

My birthday was tough those first couple of years. I sat at the niche and ate my dinner and talked to Denise. There was truly no one else I wanted to spend my birthday with more than the love of my life. Choosing to be close to her remains seemed the only thing I could do to connect to her as sad as that sounds. That first year, I even dressed up in my baby blue suit that Denise hated and offered to burn multiple times. I like to think she was laughing in heaven when she saw me in that outfit.

Birthdays were one of the times when people would reach out and connect to me to see how I was doing, but then the next day my life was empty again. I didn't handle that kind of transition well. On the practical level, I understood that people had their own lives. On the emotional level, however, I always felt abandoned.

I struggled with how to honor Denise on her birthday while also not making others sad. In the months after her passing, I sometimes posted a picture of Denise on Facebook to remind the world how beautiful she was. As time progressed, though, I wasn't sure if I should continue. I didn't want to post something on the anniversary of her passing. Although I think we should remember her that day, I preferred to commemorate her life rather than her death, so I decided that every year on her birthday, June 21, I would post one picture of her on Facebook and that would be my way to honor Denise and remind others about her. I tried to share a post that wasn't sad.

I still often spend Father's Day alone, and on Mother's Day I go to the niche and read Denise her card. As time progresses, I'm doing better.

Often, I think we fall into the trap of believing things get better with each passing day. That's a statement I myself used to make. Looking back on it, I'm ashamed that I ever made such a comment. I think I have done better every year; however, I can't claim to have improved from one day to the next. Grief is more like a seesaw that never stops with countless ups and downs. The Monday before Christmas was not half as bad as Christmas day was the first year without Denise. I have tried to encourage others who are experiencing loss by letting them know that, over time, things get better, but that doesn't mean there is improvement from one day to the next. There are always going to be situations that arise that we can't predict, and how we handle ourselves during those times speaks volumes about the people we are and the progress we make.

A group of people and families supported me on various holidays. As I reflect on those occasions, I believe I spent each of the last five Thanksgivings in a different house. As sad as I was, I did receive support. The hard part was that it wasn't always there in my day-to-day life. But there were wonderful people who reached out during the Thanksgiving holiday and brought me into their family gatherings. I'm still amazed they were willing to bring someone as depressed as I was during those times to a family gathering and just allowed me to be who I was. I am and will continue to be always grateful for those people who figured out how best to talk to me, listen to me, and help me heal.

My Christmases these days are spent doing my Denise routines before driving by myself over to see my parents. My parents continue to be amazing people and I feel bad that they have had to watch me those first couple of years. They are wonderful people and it's really nice not buying presents for myself anymore. Getting away and being around them during the holiday season was something my father had pushed for a couple of years, and I was glad I could finally deal with being away from Denise during those times.

For anyone going through struggles and tough times, holidays are so much worse. They are supposed to be filled with light and happiness, but there are so many people who don't experience those joys for a number of reasons. I am thankful I have reached a point where I am able to experience some of the joys of the holiday season. I still feel that part of the reason I seem better these days is that I'm contrasting life now with how horrible it was for so long. Going forward, holidays will probably continue to serve as a barometer for how my healing is going. I hope I reach a time when the joys outweigh the sorrows, but I never want to forget those terrible holidays.

Chapter 9
Therapy

I have always been a talker. I have also tried to always be a listener. I'm aware that sometimes the right thing has nothing to do with words as much as asking the other person what's going on and listening. I enjoy hearing others discuss their interests and describe their life experiences.

I will acknowledge that I have always relished making people smile and laugh. I clearly got this characteristic from my father, who is the most genuine, kind, helpful person I have ever known. Following in my father's footsteps gave me an unfair advantage over many people. I always wanted to be like him and had a wonderful upbringing. I was lucky to be raised by such loving parents. I know not everyone gets the kind of caring environment I grew up in, and I tried hard to never forget that.

I felt Denise and I were going to give that same type of environment to our kids, and I knew that Denise was going to be the most amazing mother. Sadly, when Denise died, that changed the trajectory of my life.

After Denise passed, I quickly started talking. My good friend Derek was kind enough to take that first week off and was around the family most of the time. He became great at reading my moods, and we took many walks those first few days. I am still shocked that he managed to remain composed on some of our walks while the emotions I expressed were so overwhelming. When Derek finally got tears in his eyes during the funeral, his own feelings became visible, but what Derek did for me that first week and continued to do meant the world to me. He gave me an outlet to pour out my emotions. Just talking and getting all the thoughts out, even the absolutely horrible and rancid ones, helped me to cope. It was much healthier to speak them than having them take up permanent residence in my head. Although I wasn't proud of many of the things I said to Derek, I felt a release as I talked to him about how much I hated the world.

As Derek got back to his job, my dad stepped in to fulfill the role of listener. We walked and talked about anything and everything. I had so much to process during those first couple of weeks, and he offered ideas and insights and helped me talk through decisions that I had to make, even though I didn't want to make any of them.

All this verbal expression was a precursor to my need for some form of therapy. I was 34 years old and a widower. I recall the first time I went to my doctor and had to fill out the updated forms, the first time I checked the "widower" box. It felt surreal, but there were so many of those firsts they just flowed together in the darkness. Anyway, at 34 and a widow, clearly I needed help, but I knew no one who could even imagine what I was going through.

My dad approached the pastor at church and asked about the Stephen Ministries organization, which provided peer counselors to assist people through difficult times with their walk of faith. The church agreed to help, and into my life walked, literally and figuratively, the amazing Mr. Bob. He reached out to me quickly after my dad approached the pastor, who knew of my situation as he sat across from me that first afternoon after Denise's passing, and we had a weird interaction where his phone made the ESPN sound. Apparently, his fantasy football team had some good news. I think the pastor was a little embarrassed because that's probably not the best time for your phone to buzz. However, we actually talked about fantasy football during those few minutes before I started crying again.

So Mr. Bob and I set up a time to start our relationship. The day he came over, I told him I think better walking, and, although Bob didn't expect and/or dress for a walk, he agreed to go with me. He and I spent many hours and miles together. We hiked through parks, around my neighborhood, and lots of different places. We also talked. Sadly, our talks weren't really happy or positive.

Bob was truly a breath of fresh air. He hadn't known Denise, but he was aware of what had happened, and we just started from there. Bob probably came to know me more during those times than my own family. We talked about everything that was going on in my head. Many times I wasn't able to face my crushing thoughts, so instead we talked about books, movies, or Bob's most adored North Carolina State (NCSU) athletics. Since Denise got her masters from NC State, I had followed their teams for a while, so we had plenty of topics to discuss on those occasions when I couldn't bear to speak about Denise or the aftermath of her passing.

Bob and I were together almost every Sunday afternoon at 3:00 p.m. He gave up watching football to walk with some guy who absolutely despised and hated the world. I honestly don't know if I could have made that type of commitment to a stranger. He regularly gave up part of his weekend to walk with me in the darkness that was my life. I feel that Bob thinks highly of me, but if he didn't there would be no shame in that. The man he encountered in those days was not the person I was before the tragedy nor the one I wanted to be. Bob met me during the worst time in my life. I really don't know how he stayed with me as long as he did. On a couple of occasions, I probably pushed him too much, and we needed to take a break from each other. I was so fragile in those days and needed someone to push me at times; I think managing my intense pain was tough on Bob. He is an incredible guy. I'm glad to say that, although we no longer take our Sunday afternoon walks, we still catch up with each other on a weekly basis.

Bob Sorrels: Stephen Minister

> *As a lay person in my church, trained in Stephen Ministry, I committed myself to God, my church, and my community to "walk" with persons through their tragedies, losses, grief, and uncertainty without judgment or personal expectations. I am not there to proselytize or convert someone's religion or beliefs but to be a kind friend and listening presence to someone in pain.*
>
> *And so, on a late October afternoon while working at the church pumpkin patch sale, I agreed to the pastor's request to meet with Levi just a week or so after his wife and twins had passed. Levi and I met that first time at his house. And, yes, he asked if we could walk while we talked. Me in my penny loafers and khaki slacks, we took off for a one hour walk/talk ending with another hour at his house. To close this first encounter, I asked if we could pray. Levi said,*

Living through my Nightmare

"Sure," and we talked to God about anger, angst, loss, and the search for meaning. This routine soon became a weekly ritual on Sunday afternoons and lasted for just over 14 months or so. (By the way I asked Santa for a new pair of Adidas walking shoes that first Christmas.)

After about a month, I decided to drive one of the routes we had walked and was astounded to discover that we were averaging 2.5 to 3.5 miles each Sunday. I listened, I reflected what I was hearing, and I empathized without implying I could even possibly relate to exactly what he was feeling. As he would often try to call me out on what I thought of his plight, I would respond with anecdotes about my own times of loss and grief in my life (like losing my father when I was six when he died in a car wreck) and how I dealt with and later compartmentalized those experiences and put them in perspectives to coincide with my faith and my view of nature and mankind. But I never suggested Levi adopt my path or strategies for reconciliation. I always reflected that he needed to find his own central core and path to reconciliation.

At his request, I did help Levi find a lawyer to talk about his hurt and anger with the medical community. We went together to that initial screening consult.

Alas, after more than a year of Sunday walks/talks, I admit that I was emotionally spent, and Levi seemed to need something more. I encouraged him to seek professional counseling or therapy. So we took some "time out" for some months. But I never gave up or divorced myself from thoughts, prayers, and concerns for this dear broken soul I had spent so much time with and had come to love as my brother (I am an only child by the way).

On a number of occasions during our walks/talks, I felt compelled to question Levi about feelings or thoughts of suicide. Though he would often say that he lived for the day to be with Denise and the twins in the hereafter, he did not go so far as to say how or by what means he might facilitate that to happen sooner rather than later. So I did not refer to crisis resources, but I stayed ever vigilant.

So now we come full circle some years after, and I started getting texts from Levi on Sunday afternoons (every Sunday afternoon without fail) asking how my week has been. I give a recap—whether positives about my grandson or NC State Wolfpack accomplishments or negatives about my wife's declining health conditions or other matters of the day. I close with "and how about you" and he recaps the same way.

I think this is Levi's way of showing me what he learned from our times and experiences together and of revealing to me the true, better Levi that he is.

I love you, Levi, as God loves you too, even if you want to be angry about why this had to happen. I pray for you to find peace, grace, love, and forgiveness in your heart and in your life. You have been and continue to be a warrior.

After Bob and I needed to take a break, I started to slip in my healing. For more than a year of walks with Bob, although I probably didn't handle myself as well as I wanted there toward the end, I knew I still truly needed someone like him to progress through my grief. Bob's work was meant to help me with my walk in faith, and clearly God and I weren't on the best of terms during those times. Bob went above and beyond what his organization asked of their ministers.

As I continued to seek outlets for healing, I remembered a text message my principal sent me about the N.C. Employee Assistance Program, which can provide various forms of support to people who are struggling.

I reached out to them and told them of my situation, explaining that, as a teacher, my hours were hard to work around. They set up an appointment with a therapist on a Saturday morning. When I first met my therapist, I thought she was warm, welcoming, and friendly. I hated the idea of trampling on her gracious nature with what I brought to the table.

She responded so well to me that we quickly developed a friendship. She is an extraordinary individual. Since we had an instant rapport, I immediately snapped up the 5:00 p.m. Thursday appointment she had available. That became my weekly appointment time every Thursday after school. I went into her office and proceeded to describe to this wonderful person how truly ugly the world was. She listened, replied as necessary, and pushed me in all the right ways. She and I became close enough that I started to ask her about herself and her family. She was willing to share about herself, and it made me feel good that I could listen to her as well as talk to her. During one of those weekly appointments that I never missed, I learned that she often had appointments lined up most of the night, which left her little time to even eat dinner. Many people who excel at their jobs get overworked, overbooked, and underpaid, which was true in her case.

I knew that wasn't exactly the healthiest thing but understood that people in her position tend to be more focused on helping others than caring for themselves. She has helped me overcome a great many hurdles and still does to this day. My world was a wreck and talking to a true professional helped.

At times during my appointments, I began with a disclaimer before I spoke openly about how I was doing. Often, I had to say, "I don't think I'm suicidal, but this is an honest thought."

Her job was to care for me, and she did that, not just because she is a therapist but because that's the type of person she is. Over time, we have laughed a lot and even developed inside jokes. Once, she was going to miss an appointment to take a much-needed and well-deserved vacation with friends to New Orleans. I told her she could only go if she had a picture taken at a head-shrinking place. Although she didn't get a photo of that, she showed one of some voodoo shop, so that seemed fair.

She was always trying to help me make connections I hadn't yet made. She would walk me through an idea or discussion, I would respond, and then she would change the subject, and I would look at her and say, "I know what you're doing." I could discern that she was trying to lead my thoughts in a particular direction, and that became a running joke.

Along with the moments of laughter and a great deal of assistance, I still shed a lot of tears in her office. As time went on, my expectations for what I had thought my life was going to be weighed more heavily on me. She helped me immeasurably to process my feelings through so many difficult situations, mind games, and painful circumstances. Nonetheless, I still held onto a huge amount of tension and frustration, many of which stemmed from the dynamics between Denise's family and me.

I am gratified that I actively and successfully attended some form of therapy since this shattering tragedy; I honestly didn't imagine I had any shot at overcoming this heartbreak without professional assistance. As far as I know, I was the only person in the situation who sought counseling. I wonder how things would have evolved if we all underwent therapy and found ways to help ourselves and each other cope with such a traumatic and inhuman loss. For my part, I was proud of my decision to seek assistance and heal my mental health issues.

I really wanted to stay close to the family of the woman I loved, but over time we grew apart. As the dynamics changed, I recognized that being around Denise's family wasn't healthy for them or for me. None of us handled everything perfectly. I was at least trying to get better, and, as part of that journey, I convinced my parents-in-law to attend a number of my therapy sessions. I felt that part of my healing was tied directly to seeing the people I wanted around me to get help too. I felt like I was losing part of Denise by being apart from her family. My therapist understood and agreed to see my parents-in-law. It took some convincing, but they finally agreed to go after a disagreement led to an ultimatum from me. I told them I would take care of the cost of the sessions, and all they had to do was show up.

I give Denise's parents all the credit in the world for attending therapy for a good while. They agreed to let me know when they were going to be there, and usually we alternated weeks. Every two weeks, I'd walk them into the room, and then I'd leave. The best support I received during those times was seeing the people around me get the help they needed.

Denise's parents and I were getting close to doing a big session together where we would really hit a lot of the tough topics, but, sadly, at this point all therapy went virtual, and we never ended up doing that. Regardless, I will forever be grateful that Denise's parents took me up on the offer of therapy.

At no point did it ever cross my mind that I could make it through all that I was up against without some form of professional help. I remember talking to people in the viewing line, saying that even script writers in Hollywood couldn't come up with an ending this cruel. This was one of the worst things I ever heard about, let alone experienced firsthand. I always felt speaking with others about the troubles and challenges was a sign of strength. One's ability to identify when he or she needs help is something we should praise, not make fun of.

Whether walking with Bob or sitting on the couch in my therapist's office, I have been given a great deal of support in trying to heal and articulate my thoughts. I wish more people attended therapy because we all deal with issues we don't want to face. I lived so much in my own head that it felt good to get another perspective from someone I value so much. Fortune may have devastated my life with an unthinkable tragedy, but I was fortunate to find fantastic people who cared and continue to help me feel my way through this turmoil.

One underrated characteristic I have going for me is my willingness to be vulnerable. I never truly tried to hide my pain. I may not want to tell someone's child that the world they live in is a cruel place, but I wasn't bothered by letting others see me for who I was during that time. My vulnerability led me to seek the help I needed and hopefully can pave the way for others down the road. I have made it through five years in a world that didn't really care how wonderful Denise and I were together or how much we would have loved those kids. I'm still here. I'm still trying. I still care.

Chapter 10

First Book

As I near the age of 40, I can reflect on what I'm most proud of in my life. It's pretty easy to identify the top three things:

1. Surviving Denise's passing
2. The first Run for Dee Dee 5K
3. Writing my first book

I hate the fact that in close to 40 years of living, the three things on this list are all a reflection of something horrific and beyond my control that I wish with every fiber of my being had never happened. It would be wonderful to look at my life and be proud of something I did that has nothing to do with seeing someone as beautiful as Denise pass away. I can't change what transpired, but if I can survive long enough to help others, then maybe what I went through can affect change.

When I was really struggling and consuming countless grief books over about nine months, I found that a number of volumes didn't speak to the rawness I was feeling. The simple idea that I might turn out okay in five years was unreal to me.

(The irony of this being a *five years after* book isn't lost on me.) I was struggling just to make it through the day at that point. How could I even imagine looking forward multiple years? The notion that things might eventually improve wasn't conceivable to the person I was then. Many of the books I read fed my belief that no one understood what I was going through. I wanted to get my hands on the book that was written by the guy who didn't make it through. At least that would have spoken to me because I knew those words would be real, and I could feel what they were feeling.

The truth is that most people enduring the kind of rawness and hopelessness I experienced during that first year are incapable of sitting down and putting words to the page that in any way explain their situation. There are probably few who have been able to do it successfully. I believe the books I read actually damaged my mental health rather than helping. I will say I got *something* out of every book, but not everything I took away from those volumes helped me. I needed a book that was filled with so much grief, anger, and hopefulness that it spoke to my life at the time. I'm sure many have attempted to write that kind of book only to have book publishers realize there isn't an audience for it. I was that audience, but I couldn't find the books that expressed my intense level of grief.

I had so many thoughts in my head, and most of them were not constructive or healthy. After my parents left for good, I really fought to figure out what to do with all those hours in the house by myself. I had gotten to the point where I could try to watch TV shows in the evenings, but the weekends were still brutal because I had way too much time and way too many detrimental thoughts in my head.

I started to consider writing the book I needed to read when I was in the thick of my anguish. I wanted to read a book that, while it might depress the average person, would let readers know there was someone else in the world who understood.

I wanted to think of a way that I could help the person I was during that first year.

The irony was that I had all the time I needed to write because I had lost everything that filled my life. I had so many hours to kill in that house alone with my thoughts and feelings, so I started inwardly debating the idea of writing the book I needed to read.

For years, I had understood the value of progress. An odd and funny example comes to mind of a sketch on *Chappelle's Show*, a TV program I used to reference frequently. In one sketch that always stuck with me, the main character discussed funny ways that he dealt with various circumstances and situations at age 18, 24, and 30. The concept of how we deal with various events at different times in our lives really spoke to me during those tough times.

I always knew that the way I would be at the one-year mark was going to be different from how I was at the three-year mark and so on. Many of those books I read were written after five years and were good for when I got to that point. But I was still in the darkest depression and desperately wanted to read something written by someone else during those dark moments.

I thought I would wait until the one-year mark to sit in front of my computer and try to write, but I didn't make it that long. I waited all summer for college football to start, but by the time it did I felt ready to start narrating my story.

Once I got the idea in my head, I struggled to think of anything else. While I was at work, ideas for the book and the topics I should discuss kept popping into my mind. As a person who makes lists for everything, I just started to write them all down. Once I had an outline of the various topics that seemed important, I started writing every weekend for a couple of months. I had been so excited about the start of college football, but its draw was diminished entirely by my calling to begin the book. I was ready to write how wonderful and breathtaking Denise was, to describe the heartbreak of finding her gone, to share the way the family pulled together that week for the viewing and funeral, and the intense journey of grief began immediately after her death. Sharing that story when it was raw served as its own kind of therapy. I needed to reveal the worst of days, the depths of my sadness, anger, and grief in hopes that someone down the road who felt crippled by grief and lost in a world that seemed foreign might find some solace in the knowing they were not alone.

I have always felt that the times in our lives when we grow and learn the most about ourselves are, unfortunately, during the really terrible periods. I discerned that I would never again be the person I was during that first year, so I wanted to put my thoughts, words, frustrations, and anger into words then in hopes that some good could come out of what I was experiencing.

Taking the notes and identifying the chapters and topics helped me to work through my grief. That first weekend of college football season, I wrote three chapters. I was exhausted afterward from bleeding emotion onto the page and trying with all my might to sound rational in the process. My brain wasn't functioning as once it had, and my thoughts remained so dark and diluted that I was unsure how the book would turn out. Nonetheless, I persevered keeping in mind that my words might someday help someone else whose life had been shattered.

One Sunday, I was so focused on putting my thoughts down on paper that I wrote four chapters in one sitting. Because I was still teaching, I just thought about topics during the weeks, put ideas down, and then wrote them and crossed out my notes on the weekends. I felt good about trying to write but also deeply regretful that the first time I ever wrote anything of substance was as a result of the worst tragedy of my life.

I had so much time alone in the house. The weekends were unbearable as I struggled to make it through the summer, but once I decided to write and began the book, I was pretty impressed with how much I accomplished. My work ethic isn't amazing, but, when I feel like something I am doing can help others, I can be dedicated and focused on the task.

I finished all the chapters by the 15-month mark after writing only on weekends. It was great therapy for me. It helped to look at many of the big picture topics I was dealing with and let the endless thoughts that circulated through my head find a place on the page. I had no idea what I would do once I was done with the writing. Although that period was when I felt the most inner anguish and chaos, it was also the time that my message and words had the most power. Few people knew how to talk to me that year, and being at home was tough. Trying to find a positive outlook, even if my words never made it into the world, was still a way to keep moving forward, processing my emotions, and spending all the hours I so desperately wanted to destroy.

I wrote the first book during a time when I thought many of the issues between Denise's family and I were going to be okay. I'm grateful to have been able to look at the positive side of my relationships with her family and friends at a time when I believed that, going forward, our sense of connection and communication would only improve. I had no desire to write anything that would hurt others, especially those who meant so much to me, so the fact that I wrote those chapters in the frame of mind that the family dynamics were going to improve helped me to honor that possibility and be true to my own desires.

Once I completed the manuscript, I had no idea what to do with it. Every three or four months, I would print and read the entire thing. I got to the point where I could skim the entire manuscript in a day. As I edited and searched for sentences that needed to be improved, I began to realize how far I had come. Putting it aside for months at a time through some really tough periods enabled me to recognize the progress I had made.

I told a couple of people about my writing and even let a few read the manuscript. I'm sure they had no idea what to say. Obviously, no one wanted to read what I wrote and say, "Wow, that's the worst thing I ever read." Ironically, that's what I wanted to hear. For me, if people recognized how tragic the story was, it would somehow validate the torment I endured during those times. I hated that my words on the page evoked tears and sadness in readers, but I was nonetheless thankful I managed to build a connection with them that came as a result of my writing.

At one point, I let my therapist read the draft and offer suggestions. She mentioned combining the two chapters I wrote about my time with Denise into one chapter because the idea was that this book detailed what happened after Denise's passing. I appreciated her suggestion to get to the heart of the book right away. Although Denise and I had a lot of wonderful memories and times together, this book was not about the years of joy. It was a reflection on the devastating death of Denise and our twins, not on the happy couple we had been.

The other suggestion she made was to go back into the chapter where I talked about finding Denise that terrible morning and describe the scene. In my first draft, I skipped from walking into the room to talking with the emergency medical personnel who told me Denise was gone from this world. I truly didn't believe people could handle what I saw in our bedroom that morning. I mean, who wants to read, watch, or hear about something as terrible and gut-wrenching as that? But my therapist was correct again. It was important to be as open and vulnerable as possible and to tell the reader the whole story. It's a shame that the story is so dark and sad, but that was the reality. I wrote that scene for the

Living through my Nightmare

person I was in that mind-altering, soul-shattering moment of complete loss.

Writing the chapters was the part I could control, which made it the simpler task in the grand scheme of creating a book. But that's only the beginning of the journey.

I asked my friend Jared to give me some suggestions for improving the manuscript. If you ever want to think of tough situations, I give you the first time I met Jared. I was in a teaching training. Like many meetings or conferences with people from other school, we guys try to stick together. Jared and I sat next to each other. Although we had never met, we got along well. The second day of the training, the presenters gave us a little time to work independently. I spent the time as I did most of the moments when I wasn't teaching: I thought about how much my life sucked and how angry I was. I crossed the room toward the library chairs by the window and started working on an email to a medical conference where I hoped to speak. (That email went unanswered and unacknowledged.) While I was reading my email draft, Jared came over and asked me about my wife. I still had on my wedding ring, so it was a natural question. Well, Jared didn't see that answer coming.

He was incredibly genuine and kind and, even after the training ended, he reached out to me, and we started corresponding. I told him about my book, and he was kind enough to read it and offer me a great deal of help with it. I'm still amazed that someone who had never met me handled my situation so well when so many people who did know me had no idea how to relate to me anymore.

Once I dealt with Jared's suggestions, I started researching agents and how to secure an agent who specialized in memoirs and then how to send in a query letter. I spent a great deal of time emailing potential agents. While I found one who looked over my chapter notes, the sad reality was that I was not unique (apart from the situation I was in), and more importantly I wasn't famous. I didn't meet the requirements for an author who is likely to earn money from a memoir. I am simply a special education teacher without a social media following. I've never been on the news or on a reality television show. My life wasn't grand enough to warrant an agent. I wasn't hurt by this. In fact, I appreciated the agents who told me that most memoirs get published because of who wrote them. Maybe I should be upset by this, but all I wanted was for someone to be real with me even if I didn't like the answer. I respected honesty and felt it was the best thing for me.

In short, there wasn't much hope for an agent, but at least I made the attempt. I may have wasted many hours, but I was grateful for something positive to spend my time on during those weekends alone.

Soon thereafter, I noticed a bulletin in the bill for my water about community news. One of the articles described a woman who had written and published a book and who was representing my small town in a positive manner. Before long, Mrs. Eagan, the woman in the article, became a teacher at my school. I asked her about her book. Mrs. Eagan wrote a delightful and popular children's book about a monkey puppet; she now goes around the country to read to kids. What a beautiful thing. She already knew my story, so I told her about my book, and she mentioned there was a guy in town with a self-publishing business. By that time the agent thing was an empty pipe dream, so I said I was completely open to that idea. That's how I met Drew Becker.

I instantly knew I would work with Drew after he asked me what I wanted out of the book, and my response was essentially that I believed my story could help others. He told me I might not make the money back that I invested in bringing the book to publication. I knew then that I would work with him. Again, I never wanted for people to tell me what they thought I wanted to hear; I needed to hear the truth. I wanted people around me who were honest and whom I could trust, and I knew I could trust Drew.

Drew did a great job of finding someone who could edit my book. Honestly, I felt horrible that anyone would have to live inside that book as well as trying to re-form my incoherent sentences, total lack of any type of writing style, and, frankly, horrible darkness. Sure enough, Diana Henderson did a fantastic job. I asked her how tough it was to read and be as involved with the book as she was, and she at once responded, "Levi, there were times that I just needed to go into the other room and pet the dog." I know I shouldn't smile at that comment, but it made me feel good to know that even someone who edits books for a living and has read many manuscripts was still affected by my story and my life.

I really doubt I will ever make my money back, but the book was never about the money; it was always about trying to help others who were suffering incomprehensible losses. I always said that if I could help one person, then it was worth it. I am happy to report that my story has helped more than one person, and I'm extremely proud that something came out of this tragedy with Denise that could assist others in their time of grief.

The first copy of my paperback book (the author's proof) that I ever received was for Denise. I like to think she helped me be the man I am, the person who was strong enough to write this story. The second copy could go to only one person: Mr. Bob. He listened as I poured out all of my dark feelings and angry beliefs during the most intensely troubled time of my life. He heard how the books I read failed to offer the solace I sought or the deep understanding of someone in the midst of their utmost pain. One of the best days I've had since that devastating day in late October 2016 was when I drove over to Bob's house after school, met him in the driveway, and handed him an envelope.

He handled it and said, "It feels like a book." Seeing Bob smile that day held special meaning. Bob had helped me open up so much, probably way more than I should have, considering how angry at the world I was. He taught me to be honest, open, and vulnerable. Those were the very qualities I needed to write the book in the first place.

Chapter 11
Religion

I have never been a deeply spiritual guy. I have lived my life believing that how we treat others speaks volumes about the type of people we are. I attended church as an adolescent, throughout college, and after college but never went as regularly as some. I always believed in karma and in doing what was right, not because I felt God wanted me to but because it was in my nature. I'm probably in the minority, but I believed strongly that God wanted us to be unselfish and to act solely from the desire to do good rather than out of a sense of obligation to a belief system.

Before I met Denise, I listened to religious podcasts weekly and continued to live a healthy and compassionate life. Although I was off and on with church, I felt I was a good person. I prayed to God to watch over me and believed that by living a wholesome and caring life I would be rewarded.

When I met Denise, we just clicked. Everything felt *right*. She attended church more than I did, and I went with her a few times. I think she always wanted to go more often, but we enjoyed our Sunday mornings together, and I usually used that time to do housework. Like me, Denise was a compassionate person, and the two of us encouraged each other's considerate, caring tendencies. I always felt that, if we became parents, we would be really good at it. I know in my heart that Denise would have been a wonderful mother.

When we found out that Denise was pregnant and that we were even luckier to be having fraternal twins, a boy and a girl, our future lives seemed almost too perfect. I remember that I prayed nightly to have healthy babies. I really didn't care about much else other than that they were healthy. I felt the two of us together would be able to nurture these tiny humans and help them become wonderful people. I expected ups and downs along the way but knew we would never take them for granted. We would have cherished them and filled their lives with much love.

When Denise passed, that life so close to perfection evaporated. I entered a world that few people experience at my age. I had a lot of questions and a great deal of anger—at the world and most certainly at God. We are so programmed to believe that God will look after us and that he can perform miracles that we may have unreasonable expectations for him. I really couldn't understand why this happened. I truly believed God had the power to help us through our difficult times. But if God could perform miracles, why was there so much sadness in the world?

What lay in store for me was far beyond my comprehension. Part of my unpreparedness stemmed from feeling that together Denise and I would make this world a better place, that we would raise our kids with love and respect, and bring a bit of grace and goodness into the lives of those we knew. On the verge of our greatest joy, those beliefs were shattered as Denise and those babies died, and for the life of me, I could not understand why. To this day, I still don't have an answer as to why this tragedy happened.

I was enraged at God for allowing this unnecessary tragedy to happen. Why would I ever put my faith in him again? The fact that I allowed Denise's remains to be housed at a church seemed insane given my anger. But somehow my heart knew it was the best place for her, where she would want to be, and I'm glad she is there. I'm also grateful that I was able to go to church regularly and sit with Denise's parents.

Even so, I needed to know why this tragedy came to pass. As much and as often as I had prayed for healthy babies before Denise passed, I pleaded with God to understand why this happened after she died. Just having Denise's water break would have been enough of a miracle for me. That's all that I needed God to do. Sadly, he sat idly by and watched Denise and those babies leave this world before our twins even got to take their first breath.

Although I continued to struggle with God's role in this loss and my subsequent depression, I acknowledged the kindnesses the church showed to Denise's family and me. We held the viewing and the funeral there, and they were extremely accommodating and clearly cared for our well-being. The pastors showed compassion and gave me the great gift of connecting me with Mr. Bob. They also provided a grief share class to help us through an immeasurably difficult time and served as a wonderful support to Denise's family and me when we needed all the help we could get.

After Denise's passing, I felt oddly connected to the church even though I was still exceedingly angry with God. I was pleased to know that Denise's remains were placed with such care in a beautiful location so close to the house. Denise's parents and I attended the church regularly and always arrived early. I'd put my bottled water and my lumbar roll (small back pillow) down inside and then grab a folding chair and head back outside to the columbarium to talk to Denise. Week after week, I repeated the same ritual. It was what I needed to do, but I still felt the irony of spending so much time in a place where people were rejoicing while believing that everyone in that sanctuary seemed to praise a false hope. I don't mean to say that's what God is. I mean to say that sometimes we believe that bad things won't happen to us because God won't allow them to. That's the false hope. Terrible things are always going to happen—no matter how good a person you are. Sometimes the better you are, the more unprepared you are because you believe that being a good person matters in the greater scheme of life.

I repeatedly asked myself why this happened to us. The only helpful thought I had was that, maybe, because I had the necessary tools and was the type of person who could make it through this terrible tragedy, I was the one who experienced it. That may sound arrogant, but that isn't my intention. That's just the only rational reason I ever came up with. However, my response to that was, "Just because I *could* handle the pain doesn't mean I should have to."

I will always wonder why God didn't just take my life rather than Denise's. I mean, if someone was going to die in our family, it should have been me. Although it would have been incredibly tough for Denise, I firmly believe that, with those kids, she could have lived a meaningful life. She was an extraordinary woman, one who deserved to live. God should have watched over her and those twins instead of letting them die.

Sitting outside by Denise's urn during all the important holidays seemed to be the only fitting thing to do, but the fact she wasn't there in the physical world beside me was still incomprehensible. I never really understood why this anti-miracle was allowed to take place, but it forced me to question so much about the world and myself.

Early on after Denise's passing, when I was only in the house for a little bit of time, I got a knock on the door. A couple of pastors who I'm sure got a list of all the new residents in the area had come to invite Denise and me to their church. I informed them that it was just me and then told them why. The pastors handled themselves as well as they could have and then offered to pray for me. I really, really, *really* wanted to turn to them and say, "Why? I prayed for healthy babies, and look where that got me. Why would we think prayer works now?"

I know that sounds unpleasant, but that's how I felt at the time. Even though I'm not as raw as I was then, I still question God's role in this. Instead of crushing their spiritual intentions, I just let them pray, and then they went on their way. It was probably the kindest thing I could have done. By letting other people live their lives, I avoided drawing them down into my darkness. Maybe during those times, I should have been more open about my feelings related to how dark the world was, but that was neither the time nor the place to be *that* person.

At one point someone at church who knew my story approached me and asked for my help. This polite man let me know that someone in his family had lost his wife. He was a young guy, maybe in his late 20s, whose his wife had gone in for a dangerous and invasive procedure and had not made it through the surgery. As you might expect, this gentleman wasn't handling it well. I could deeply relate to the situation, so this churchgoer asked if I would reach out to him. I said I would be more than happy to because, as bad off as I was, I still wanted to help others as much as I could. I sent him a couple of texts but never heard back. I wasn't disappointed; I just wanted to do my part to help someone else.

A little over a year later, I asked the churchgoer how his relative was, and he replied that he wasn't doing well. He was living in his parent's basement and playing video games all day. I turned to him and said, "But he's alive, right?"

The man just looked at me, and then he got it. He understood that someone couldn't simply move on from something like this, that the fact he was even alive was more than some people might manage. It was going to be in that boat with him for a while. After I mentioned my side of it to him, the man at church sincerely thanked me for showing him the side of the situation he was missing. It felt good to help another person recognize the level of sorrow that comes with this kind of tragedy.

Going to church as much as I did, I often had to face all those happy people with their happy lives. Hearing all the joyful, upbeat praise every week was pretty torturous. While I understood the value of putting myself in the thick of it, seeing people have faith in something I didn't fully believe in was difficult for me. But I was never going to make it through if I couldn't face the hard moments. There were times when I struggled not to cry in front of people during the service. There were even more times while I sat by Denise's remains that I was absolutely a wreck. I'd cry so much I had snot running down my nose and then I'd walk into the church and people would just look at the mess that I was. That's who I was during that time of my life and to shy away or try to hide wasn't healthy. Being able to be as close to Denise as I could, but also listening to scripture and sermons about how great God is was tough, but it was the only way I could face my uphill climb.

As my relationship with Denise's parents became more distant, I started sitting in the back of the sanctuary by myself. I often drove solo to church, put down my things, and then headed back outside and talk to Denise. When I returned from those visits, there were fewer seats open. Thankfully, the ushers knew me and my story. I had helped them on a number of occasions to retrieve more chairs and escort other people to available seats. I just needed to be close to Denise. Being in the sanctuary around a lot of people was a step in the right direction.

On one occasion, when I returned inside after talking and crying with Denise, one of the ushers joked that he didn't know if I was coming back. I realized he didn't know my story. When I explained where I had been and why, I caught him off guard. I already wasn't in the most chipper of moods, and his obvious discomfort after I told him sent me into a tailspin. Rather than being kind, he just sort of laughed one of those excruciating laughs that escape people's mouths when they feel horrified. Although I knew what happened and why, in that moment I couldn't pretend that hideous response was okay. I just said, "I don't find it funny," and walked away.

It was Palm Sunday, and after the service I went out to talk to Denise again. Someone had taken one of the palm branches and wedged it up on Denise's niche. I didn't know it was him, but I *knew* it was him. It was his way of acknowledging that he was sorry for his previous response. After that, whenever we saw each other, we just nodded to each other. How he handled himself initially was abhorrent, but I believe the kindness he later showed spoke to his true character.

There were other exchanges that happened with people through church. I was running one day around my neighborhood and saw a man and woman jogging. The first time I ran by them, the woman looked at me like I was trash. I had no idea what I did to her, but her face said it must have been something bad. After a couple more miles, I passed them again, and oddly she spoke to me. We ended up talking for about 10 minutes, and I began to get that uncomfortable feeling that I was about to turn their day south. She asked why running was so important to me, and, before I could reply that it helped my mental health, the man, who was now running behind us, said, "I already told her about you." I was so relieved. He informed me that he knew of me from church, which made me feel so much better. The church was filled with caring people. As much as I hated how uncomfortable I felt with a lot of the symbolism and messaging, I knew the people were kind and compassionate.

After about three and a half years, the church announced that we would be getting new pastors. Our ministers, who had been wonderful to me, were moving on. When the new ones came, both the male and female pastors were about my age. Usually, I envision ministers being old and wise, but these two were young and seemed to be highly intelligent.

I didn't approach either of them because they had a lot on their plates with meeting everyone and trying to keep track of names and all that comes with being new to the congregation. However, there was one exchange that will stay with me forever.

I was sitting outside talking to Denise when Owen, the lead pastor, walks by me and says, "Just know you're not alone out here."

I turned and looked at him and said, "You know my story."

Owen replied with the single most perfect response I could ever have imagined. He said, "I know enough for it to be dangerous."

He didn't pretend to understand how I was doing. He just said that he knew enough for it to be dangerous. Those words touched my core.

I have become close to Owen because we are both about the same age and have similar interests. However, I'm sure that when he sees me he recognizes how lucky he is. I'm lucky to call Owen my friend.

We have had many talks, and he is always there for me. He asked me to please give him a heads up if I ever felt the need to shout out objections during a sermon. He realizes that a lot of what I hear makes me angry and raises more questions, but we both recognize that often the sermons are not written for me. Even so, he gives me plenty to think about, and knowing that he understands my situation makes it much easier to tune in during his sermons.

As I attempted to grow spiritually, over time I have gotten better, and my bitterness toward the universe has lessened. I'm still not best friends with God, but I'm not enemies with him either.

I have found the other pastor, Hope, caring and easy to talk to. I mentioned to her once that it might be time for me to join the church. She knew this was a huge consideration for someone like me. I attended a little seminar about becoming a member, but then Hope and I had a sit-down. The church has certain questions that prospective members need to answer, and, frankly, I still wasn't prepared to respond to a couple of those. I still struggled with the whole idea that God is our savior and is always there for us. My life and Denise's death revealed something different. Thankfully, Hope was all right just asking the questions I felt comfortable answering.

She also mentioned coming forward to join during a service. Beyond the fact that I attend, I didn't really need everyone to know of my involvement with the church. However, I understood the value of people seeing that the church was still growing. I said I'd be more than happy to participate but that I would rather do so during the early service, which is often much less populated. She asked if I wanted someone with me, and, of course, for me that person was Mr. Bob.

We put everything in place for me to join the church officially. Then, the pandemic happened, church was canceled, and everything went virtual. When I was extremely close to finally joining, the coronavirus came and once again I was home alone.

I didn't go to church. I didn't see Denise weekly. I listened to religious podcasts but everything changed. I had to adjust. It was a weird but interesting time for me. In some respects, it was good and in others not. Instead of driving to church, on Sunday mornings I took a long walk and did some reading.

I ended up not joining the church after being a breath away from doing so. I still listen to podcasts of sermons, and, if something catches my ear, I text Owen and tell him about what I thought of his discourse. It's not the same as being there, but at least I still visit Denise, and I will always be thankful for how that church treated me back when I was struggling and at my worst.

Probably the best way to explain my growth was with something that happened during my July planning days at school. I was in a teacher meeting because that's what happens to teachers when you're not with kids, and I got a call to come to the office. Outside the office stood a friend whom I hadn't seen for years.

The year Denise passed was the first year I didn't get to work with a wonderful teacher named Ashley. She had become pregnant and had taken a break from teaching. The last time I saw her was during Denise's viewing. Ashley brought her two kids, whom I had never met until then. Now, here she was, just this happy, smiling person waiting to see me. There were probably 40 different teachers and staff members she could have visited that July day. But she showed up and wanted to see me. I was honored that she took the time out of her busy life to visit me.

She wanted to know how I was doing. She had felt guilty after reading my book. She thought she should have done more for me. I told her I had no ill feelings toward her and that I always knew she cared. But because she is such a caring and reflective person, she still believed she needed to do more.

Ashley had something wrapped that clearly was a picture frame. She wasn't sure what kind of state I was in, so she asked how I felt about pictures of Denise. I told her I was comfortable looking at pictures of Denise and that over time I had gotten much better at gazing again at Denise's loving smile. I unwrapped the gift and found a beautiful colored painting of Denise holding the twins with me and with Jesus between the two of us. I had no idea what to say. It was incredibly kind and such a wonderful painting. Ashley had gone to the trouble of getting photos of Denise and me and have someone paint them. No words could have described my gratitude for this precious remembrance.

I brought the painting home and hung it. I value it for its artistry, for the kindness my friend showed by offering such a gift, and as a symbol of the fact that I have grown enough spiritually to look at the religious aspect of it and still see the beauty. I don't think I could have done that previously. What Ashley did was so generous and kind, and her visit out of the blue with that present demonstrated what a caring friend she is.

I keep the picture in my bedroom and gaze at it every morning and night. Although God and I aren't on the same terms we once were, and may never be, I'm grateful for this loving gift. God failed to intervene on behalf of the most wonderful woman who had waited all her life to become a mother. Instead, she left this world without ever holding her babies in her arms.

I value people who are spiritual. Those who have lost loved ones and have remained close to God reveal an inner strength that is a credit to them. They are much stronger than I am.

For the life of me, I will never understand why this tragedy happened. I don't know if God is to blame, but I think God had the power to prevent it and didn't. I don't know if I will ever get over that fact.

When I pray at night these days, I ask God to look after my friends and family, but I don't ask him to watch over me. Denise does that for me. Maybe someday I'll see God as I once did before my life was altered beyond belief. Unfortunately for Denise's friends, family, and for me, God did not intervene when we needed him to.

Chapter 12
Medical Community

I may never get the answers I need regarding God's role in Denise's death. But we didn't pay God to look after her health. We compensated the doctors to care for her in that regard.

The facts remain that twice, two different doctors saw a 39-year-old, at-risk patient who carried two full-term twins during the week before her death. Denise was worried about her health. She expressed her concerns to me one night before bed. I did what I thought was the responsible thing and reminded her of all those people who never became pregnant. I'm comfortable saying with certainty that Denise expressed her fears to the two doctors she saw before she passed. I couldn't attend those appointments because I was at school working, but I believe she mentioned it because I saw how Denise reacted after her last appointment.

When I met Denise at her paranatal appointments, which were immediately after her OB/GYN visits, I saw her cry a number of times. In the early part of her pregnancy, her feelings stemmed from the bedside manner of many of the doctors who saw her. On a few occasions, Denise was smiling from ear to ear after her visit. I knew then that she had seen the one doctor there whom she loved. He was a kind and gentle man who made her feel at ease.

As she continued to progress to full-term, Denise was still affected by how she was treated, but, much more concerning, she was worried about her own safety. So was my mother-in-law, who went with her to a couple of doctor visits. Of course, we were not medical professionals. We put our trust and our lives in the hands of these doctors, and sometimes they get it wrong. In this case, they were dead wrong.

I still believe that even if I had gone into her doctor's office and made a scene, they might not have induced her. But if I had done that, I would have had a lot fewer sleepless nights. When Denise died, I was left picking up the pieces.

I'm sure those doctors felt remorseful. I have to be careful here because of the legal implications. I know they were regretful about Denise's death. I'm not saying they did something wrong. In today's society, sometimes we do not accept accountability for our actions for fear of liability and lawsuits. Sadly, that was the big issue that we encountered.

The idea that my wife died under their care made it impossible for them to reach out to support me. I found support in other ways, but that doctors' office made the decision not to be there for me because of a potential lawsuit.

My role was to love Denise and to help her as much as I could. I gave her the affection and care that any loving husband would. However, Denise died in our house from a brain hemorrhage, and I alone was left to deal with all that followed, to call the emergency personnel, to talk to the police. However, I wasn't her doctor. Her physicians should have been the ones to relate what happened to her. To have the police essentially question me shows how crazy the system is. I loved Denise and I treated her like a queen. I don't believe Denise felt the medical personnel in her OB/GYN office provided her with the kind of regard or care she needed, yet the authorities never questioned them. The doctors never had to explain their care to anyone, and that still doesn't sit right with me.

A simple card arrived from their office after Denise's passing. In contrast, my personal doctor called and wanted me to come in, and the staff from her other doctors' office, who did her paranatal care, sent a special card in which multiple people wrote something from the heart. The day I went to their office to thank them for the meaningful card was a tough one. I knew they would be busy, but I needed to let them know how much their compassion meant to me during those moments of torment. They treated me like a person, and I will never forget how kind they were to Denise before her death and how sympathetic they were to me after she passed. Those people showed me there is a way.

However, the OB/GYN staff thought that a blanket card was all they could do at that time. I am absolutely sure they wanted to do more, but, because of legalities, their administration or their lawyers told them not to. Such situations reveal much about a business and the people in that business.

The day I went to pick up her medical documentation from the OB/GYN office was a strange day. I scheduled a pickup and told them what I needed, and they had the documents ready for me. After I picked them up, I went to my personal physician and got my blood drawn because my doctor was worried about my health. Afterward, I looked over the documentation in my car. I didn't understand all the vocabulary and notes, but I noticed one thing: Nowhere in any of the documentation was there even the slightest mention of Denise being concerned about her health. That's when I realized this might be a dirty business. I understand it is a business, but I also think we should care what people think about themselves. We are all more than just data, even though data drives conclusions or, in this sad case, what drove them not to make the decision to induce labor.

I will always remember that day I read through those files. After having blood drawn, I needed to get some food and wanted to see how I would handle being in a public place. I ended up crying as I ate my breakfast sandwich, so needless to say I wasn't able to function in a public forum by myself yet.

Recalling that time, I can't tell you how angry I was. I had so many sleepless nights wondering how this could have happened. Denise and I had sat through all the meetings because she was having an "at-risk" pregnancy only to end up in a situation we couldn't control. It was incredibly heartbreaking, and I have never experienced that degree of anger, which stayed with me for so long.

I needed to know that those doctors and staff members who worked at that OB/GYN cared about my survival, to get some sense that they didn't want me to commit suicide and that I was more important than money. Sadly, instead of seeing me as a grieving person who needed their help, they viewed me as a potential lawsuit. That fact forever changed how I view the medical community.

I never expected them to call me and bring me in and say this is where we went wrong, but I imagined they might let me know they cared and understood that what I was going through was overwhelming. Instead, they showed me they cared more about their money than about my life. I was more than a potential lawsuit. I was a person desperately in need of help. Sadly, the world I entered when Denise died was not the one I had known all my life.

Living through my Nightmare

When I woke up at night and wasn't able to get back to sleep, I imagined the people at that office slumbering in their beds and going on with their wonderful lives. The fact that I had to take medication to get any rest and still couldn't sleep through the night didn't matter. I had trusted God and the medical community and neither seemed to care. When it all went south, they hung me out to dry. I can't tell you how angry I was. I felt those doctors' behavior reflected poorly not only on that business but on the entire medical community.

I do not believe that all places would deal with those situations in the same way but, for better or worse, that OB/GYN office is a symbol of the medical community, and their staff clearly didn't represent it in a way that anyone would be proud of.

I was fortunate to have a neighbor who knew an OB/GYN who came to talk to me one night. She was a kind woman and helped me understand that the data really didn't show that Denise's condition was as dire as I assumed. This wonderful person even admitted that, had she been the doctor caring for Denise, she might have continued to wait until Denise's water broke or she was even farther along. Denise was already 36 weeks pregnant, but hearing this honesty from an impartial OB/GYN made me feel that maybe it wasn't entirely a horrible mistake. I still felt my wife's death should never have happened, but perhaps her doctor's actions weren't as careless as I had assumed.

Shortly thereafter, I started to feel disappointed in myself for how angry I had become at everyone in the medical community. I needed to be smarter about how I conducted myself. The first thing I did was to write a letter to the older male doctor whom Denise had loved because I felt certain he had truly cared for her as a patient and a person. I also wrote thank-you notes to my own doctor and to the OB/GYN who helped me understand some of the data. I didn't want my views regarding that one office to define my feelings about the entire medical community. A number of people who work in this field are dedicated professionals, and it would be wrong to think of them all as uncaring. The reality was that my intense anger and distress clouded my ability to think rationally. As time went on, I could separate that single OB/GYN office and their staff from the rest of the medical community. Writing that first thank-you letter to the male doctor helped me to get my head back to a rational place. Under the circumstances, I doubt many people would have sent that note, but doing so returned me to my center, which was what I desperately needed.

While I was still investigating what happened and what steps should be taken, I met with a lawyer who was someone the family knew of. It was important to hear the legal side of this tragedy but caused additional sorrow as well when I was told that, although their three lives were lost, there was only one social security number and, therefore, essentially only one death. In a time when there is so much debate about abortion, I was floored by this news. It seemed like those kids didn't matter to anyone. Well, they mattered to the family, to Denise, and to me. But the state didn't care about the fact that they were full-term. That news brought home the fact that finding a way to make sure this never happened again was going to be challenging.

The lawyer was polite and informative but clearly wasn't interested in our case. After at least a couple of months without contact from him, I had to reach out to him again only to be informed that he was not going to take the case. He was more interested in referring clients to other lawyers who were a good match and had tried unsuccessfully to find someone to take our case. After waiting so long to hear from him and losing many hours of sleep in the interim, receiving the news of his decision was really difficult. I found it challenging to deal with the business side of death when I was still enmeshed in life-altering sadness.

Living through my Nightmare

I met with a second lawyer, who seemed much more personable and compassionate. He informed me that sometimes the nurse's notes are the more important documentation because doctors don't often elaborate much in their notes for just these types of occasions. However, a doctor's office doesn't have to share nurse's notes, and you better believe I never saw a single nurse's note. The system is what the system is. With only the data that we had, this attorney decided not to take the case either.

About a day after he let me know, I sent him a follow-up email, asking if he would have taken the case if any red flags showed up in the notes. I felt uncomfortable that we use doctors' notes against them, which actually encourages them not to document how a patient feels. It seems incredibly near-sighted, but this is big business and money is at stake. I never heard back from the attorney in response to my question, but to be fair in his shoes I probably wouldn't have responded either. Whatever his answer might have been, the fact remained that the data didn't show a mistake.

The third lawyer with whom I met also didn't take the case, which was what I expected by this point. The rules seemed to be in place to cover the doctors, not the patients, or maybe this was just a freak accident. I still don't have a clue. I only know that my beautiful, beloved wife should never have died.

Finally, an additional lawyer talked me through everything and told me how tough these lawsuits were because it's hard to prove much in these cases. Since he refused to take the case, I felt I could trust everything he said. This attorney was impressed by the fact that I was about to have a sitdown with two doctors from the OB/GYN office.

After almost a year of hating the world, I couldn't go on like that. I made a phone call to the OB/GYN office and asked for a meeting. I just wanted to get in a room with them. Surprisingly, they agreed and I found myself sitting in a room with the wonderful male doctor who treated Denise so well, the one to whom I had written a thank-you letter, as well as the female doctor who was the last to see Denise.

Getting in a room with these two, having them see me for who I was, was probably the best thing for my mental wellbeing. I ended up crying on the shoulder of the male doctor. They said what they said, and, while I didn't agree with everything, at least they *saw* me. They treated me like a person. That was the first time anyone from that office showed me the care and grace that we want from fellow human beings, let alone doctors. In their eyes I sensed a desire to have done more for me earlier in my grief, but they were not able to. These two wonderful people were censored by policy and not able to show how caring and nurturing they could be to someone in my situation. Before I asked for that meeting, I honestly felt that it was better for the staff in that office if I committed suicide. I'm sure they wouldn't have wanted that, but their lack of kindness at the worst time in my life left me feeling further isolated.

I'm so thankful that I kept living for that year and will forever be grateful that they agreed to see me. Those doctors sat with me, cried with me, and showed me there is a better way to handle the tragedy than they did the previous year.

After the meeting, true to my character, I wrote them each a thank-you letter. I didn't expect to form a friendship with these doctors, but I was so appreciative that they took the time to show me compassion. I hoped that if this situation ever presented itself again, they would handle it differently after having met me. Hopefully, they will never lose another patient. I am forever thankful for the grace they finally showed me.

After returning home from a vacation a few weeks after my meeting with the doctors, I found a letter sent to me by the female doctor. That might be the single most impactful letter I ever received. She explained how profoundly affected she was by meeting me and said how much she took away from hearing me talk. She told me how hard it was for her not to be able to reach out to me and added that she would try to find a way to provide support to someone in my position if the situation ever happened again. She showed a great deal of compassion. This was the first time that anyone in that office was proactive and not reactive. I had initiated the meeting when clearly they weren't going to ask me to come in on their own. However, this letter proved to me that she truly cared and that my words had been powerful, that they had affected her. I felt reassured that someone in that office made an effort to set things right.

One afternoon, I was watching a movie that had forgiveness as a major theme. The main character went to many people, forgave them, and then apologized for some of his own actions. As I viewed the film, I began to notice anxiety building inside me. By this point I was really good at reading my body. I paused the movie, went into the spare bedroom, curled into the fetal position, and just cried. At that moment I knew that I needed to forgive Denise's doctors.

I understood the value of forgiveness and, most importantly, I comprehended how important it was for my mental health. I agreed then and there that I would forgive them for whatever mistakes they had made. But there was a part of me that wasn't ready to forgive how they treated me after Denise's death. That was the moment I realized my issue was not with doctors; it was with the administration and the business side, with the people who signed their checks. The callousness of the business aspect of medicine might be the downfall of the medical community. I hated that I had to learn that truth in this way. Lying there on the floor, the tears poured out of me, offering a welcome release. I had to let go of my anger at doctors. They did what they did, and, yes, they should have listened to Denise, but her death was not the ending anyone wanted, including her doctors. Sometimes the data says everything is fine, and every once in a while the data is wrong.

Over time things got better in my life. Therapy continued to be instrumental. My therapist and I had a lot of talks about how we could change the system. Most places still don't want to acknowledge the kind of issue that happened to Denise, and I didn't know how to prevent this situation from recurring.

One afternoon, I decided to write and post a Yelp review because I think it's important to be honest and wanted to prevent another tragedy. A couple of days later, my review seemed to disappear under other older ones. When I emailed Yelp, they explained that their "algorithm" was the reason it appeared lower down in the list even though it was the most recent. The guy I emailed just kept saying the algorithm was the problem, but he wasn't going to change it. I think my line to him was, "I don't think I need to say how I had a good meal at Chipotle to get people to know that my wife died under the care of this place," but apparently even those words couldn't alter their policy. Another example of the world not caring.

Emotional triggers arise in strange ways sometimes. One of the more unique examples happened while I watched a documentary about a failed music festival. The lawyer who didn't reply to my "red flag" email appeared in the film. I guess he had enough time to sit for this filming but not enough to email a response to someone who lost his wife and kids. That seemed par for the course for my life.

Despite dealing with occasional situations that provoke a dive into the darkness, I'm proud of the progress I've made. My anger has diminished and no longer consumes me. After five years, I still can't imagine why Denise had to die. Because she was full-term, I think everyone can agree that this was preventable. I'm glad that her doctors agreed to meet with me so that I could begin to see physicians as good people again. I believe the business side of that office was the actual issue and feel certain they could and would have handled this completely differently if one of their own family members were involved. But I'm pleased that I no longer become so angry when I mention the doctors who saw Denise. I do still feel that a conversation needs to be had with members of the administration who didn't care for my survival. Acknowledging that belief was the reason I called and attempted to schedule a meeting with the administration at the OB/GYN office. After I left that message, I received the letter from their lawyers.

Chapter 13

Law

It took me a couple of years, but I finally was able to funnel my frustration into what really made me angry. Yes, I was angry that Denise passed, but, beyond that, I felt the same thing could happen again. This could have happened to any patient and to any doctor. The data said Denise wasn't in immediate danger, she felt that she was, and the decision was made not to induce her. I expect this type of disagreement happens pretty regularly. Sadly, this time it led to the death of the woman I loved and our twins. Denise didn't deserve to die. The fact that she never got to hold those babies remains a tragedy. The system failed my wife and our children. While I couldn't alter the past and change this mistake, I was deeply concerned that it could happen again. After I met with two of her doctors and they showed me the compassion I had waited to receive, my life and mental health improved. However, as time went on, I realized the need to sit down with the administration as well. Although I can forgive the mistake of not inducing Denise,

I can't forgive how they treated me after the mistake, or at least I can't until they understood how they failed me as a person.

When I called the first time to make an appointment with the administrator, I was informed there was a new administrator, so I figured I would need to inform this person of the situation. Luckily, the person didn't pick up. I still don't enjoy blindsiding people when I ask for these types of meetings. However, the downside of voicemail is that you can only leave a brief message, and mine wasn't short. I tried to explain everything, but I couldn't get in all the details. I had to leave a second shorter message, essentially asking for a sit-down with the administration. I said they could bring the doctors, their lawyers, or anyone they wanted to. I just knew I needed to get in a room with them for my mental health and so that I could see the medical community in a way that was positive.

I got a response a couple of days later saying that the two doctors who already met with me would be happy to sit down with me again. My first thought was that this was not what I asked for. I didn't understand how I wasn't being clear. If they wanted to join the meeting, they were more than welcome, but the primary person I needed to meet was the administrator. My issue was with the business side, not the doctors. I felt certain the administration had instructed the doctors not to contact me during my time of grief. That's the real conversation I needed to have.

I called them back and left a message again, informing them that I appreciated the doctors being willing to meet with me, but I wanted and needed to talk to the administration. I hoped my second message was clearer.

About a week later, immediately after my weekly therapy appointment, I pulled my car into the mail kiosk and found a couple of letters from some law firm. I opened them as soon as

Living through my Nightmare

I got in the house. One letter had been sent to the old address and forwarded; the other had come to the new house. They were both identical and they read:

> Dear Mr. Moore:
>
> *I have been retained by (the name of the doctors' practice) to represent it in connection with your repeated requests to meet with physicians and staff members to discuss your wife's care. It is my understanding that (the name of the female doctor) and (the name of the male doctor) met with you previously on October 31, 2017, to provide you with copies of Mrs. Moore's medical records, discuss her care and treatment at (medical practice name), and answer any questions you had at the time. Since that meeting, the practice has received letters and photographs from you and/or your family members expressing feelings of ill-will toward the physicians and staff at (doctors' office name). I understand that you are now requesting an additional meeting with members of the administrative staff who were not involved in your wife's medical care. Per my advice, (doctors' office name) respectfully declines this meeting: (the name of the male doctor) and (the name of the female doctor) have already explained in detail the care and treatment provided to Mrs. Moore and answered your questions. (The practice)'s physicians and administrative staff have no further information to offer you.*
>
> *Further, after receipt of the letters and photographs, the physicians and staff at (the practice*

name) have become concerned about your behavior; therefore, I am writing to ask that you not contact (practice name) again. I have instructed (practice name) not to take your phone calls. I have also instructed (practice name) to call law enforcement if your phone calls persist or if you visit the practice.

While (female doctor), (male doctor), and all of the physicians and staff at (practice name) remain truly sympathetic to your loss and grief, your actions and statements have raised concerns for (practice name) employees as well as other patients and their families. We hope that you understand and will respect these boundaries.

Sincerely,

(Lawyer's name)

To say that this made me incredibly angry would be underselling my feelings. I couldn't believe how rude, disrespectful, and unsympathetic this was. I buried my wife and unborn twins, who relied on their organization to look after them, and here this medical practice was having lawyers write this to a widower still trying to reconcile unspeakable grief.

I waited a year before asking for a meeting. I was extremely polite and caring when I sat down with two of Denise's doctors. I wrote thank-you letters to these people afterward. I had no idea what they were talking about regarding letters and photos

Living through my Nightmare

expressing "ill will." At this point, I truly wanted to punch a wall. They could have simply said, "No, we can't meet with you," but instead they chose to threaten me with bringing in the police if I called again.

I was in shock. What kind of human would act like this to someone going through what I was experiencing? I stood there in my empty house, longing for someone to talk to. I tried to call my therapist immediately, but she was already with her next client and didn't pick up. I ended up calling Pastor Owen, who clearly walked into a conversation with a guy that wanted to fight someone and had every single reason to be absolutely angry.

Owen did the best he could and was able to calm me down to a point where I wasn't afraid I was going to put my fist through a wall. We both knew there was nothing he could do for me apart from letting me vent. He was nothing but gracious to me. I just couldn't believe anyone would send something so callous to someone in my shoes. Of everyone involved, I believe I acted with the greatest care and maturity, and here they were accusing me of harassing them. After I vented sufficiently to get my emotions under control, I told Owen that he wouldn't need to worry that I would be like this again.

That night, I got maybe three hours of sleep and wasn't able to sleep through the night for about four nights. By then, things started to become clear. Friday, the next day, I emailed the lawyer to try to understand what in the world she was talking about. I omitted my thoughts about them attempting to control the narrative and flip the responsibility onto me. Instead of the administrator responding to my first voicemail in a way that made sense, they left me thinking I hadn't been clear enough, which prompted me to call again. All they had to do was call me and either schedule a meeting with me, clarify what I needed, or let me know they had no intention of seeing me. Instead, they had an attorney draft that letter. A truly disrespectful move but it was a great way to take no accountability. I had lost my future and my world, but rather than face me, they chose to turn my need for understanding and compassion against me. What a horrible and cruel way to go about "business."

The letter was so strongly worded that I felt concern for my reputation should they ever send the authorities to speak to me, so I decided to share what happened with my principal. I believe she had just returned from a viewing or funeral for someone who had passed away when I asked to speak to her privately the day after I received the letter. We went into her office and shut the door. A couple of other administrative staff members were there, so I said they were welcome to join us. I felt the more ears, the better.

I will never forget that moment, leaning against the wall and watching my principal read that letter in a chair next to the door. She looked at me and asked what happened, and I had no idea what to tell her. She passed the letter to let the other people read it, and I just told them I asked for a meeting with the administration, and they told me I could meet with the same two doctors again; I called back to say I wanted to see the administrator. That's literally all I knew. I didn't feel I did anything wrong.

I didn't know what to tell my school administration, and I'm sure they had no idea what to say to me. I wanted to be honest with them because, whenever one gets a letter that talks about getting law enforcement involved, I feel it's important to be honest with one's bosses. We left it at that and I'm sure they walked out of that meeting wondering what had happened because they all know me and my character, and something clearly didn't match up.

By the end of the day, I didn't hear from the lawyer, so I assumed it would be Monday at the earliest before I received some form of answer.

Over the weekend, I texted Denise's parents, whom I wasn't seeing regularly at that time. I mentioned the letter from the lawyer in hopes they could shed some light on the situation. Denise's father admitted that at the one-year mark, probably after I met with the doctors, he wrote a letter to the practice.

I told him it wasn't a big deal, even though I knew it was. Denise's father had cared for me after she died. He put his hand on my back that first night when I cried so hard, and, day in and day out, he showed that he cared about my survival, my mental health, and how I was doing. I knew he would feel terrible that they used his poor decision to continue to avoid me on an administrative level. I understood her father sent that letter to make himself feel better. Like all of us, he struggled so much that first year. Like any grieving father might have done, he decided to vent to the practice in a letter, and they, in turn, used his decision to keep me from getting more closure. After he explained, I just went on about my day and didn't make it out to the big deal that it was.

On Monday, when I got the email response from the lawyer, she showed me what he had sent. It was a typed narrative of the babies asking Denise in heaven why everyone on earth was able to have cake and they weren't. It was a sweet narrative, but the other part of the letter was probably more unnerving.

Denise's father had sent a photo of the babies, the only one we have, which was taken at the funeral home, along with a handwritten note. In the anonymous note, he said that Denise and the babies died because the doctors had failed to listen to her. He added that they should put a copy of the picture of the babies in their desk drawers so this didn't happen again. He ended the letter with the line, "There is no forgiveness in our hearts for any of your doctors." Those were powerful words, but, taken out of context, they were also concerning. The letter my father-in-law wrote showed how much pain we all were in. While he shouldn't have sent the letter, a grieving father will do what he has to, and I understood that he wrote it in the hope that they wouldn't let this happen to another family.

The fact remained that the letter from the lawyers was aimed at me and my "behavior" even though I did not send the photo or the letter and had no knowledge of them until after the fact. I shouldn't have been penalized for the actions of others.

I went back and forth via email with the lawyer over the severity of her letter to me, and, although she tried to be kind and sympathetic, she was never going to give me the meeting with the administrator that I initially sought.

I felt strongly that, before sending such a letter as the one I received, the attorney should have known *for certain* that I had some involvement in the letter and photograph. Their aggressive wording led me to believe that they felt I wrote the letter that Denise's father actually sent or had some involvement in it. If they had checked the handwriting and compared it to my thank-you notes to two of their doctors, they would have seen the two looked nothing alike. But this would have required due diligence and behaving like humans instead of simply a business. I went back and forth on this point with the lawyer a number of times.

When my principal asked how the situation was resolving, I explained about Denise's father's letter and photo and described my back and forth with the lawyer which was like playing chess. The attorney came really hard out of the gate with her queen, but I took it and now I wanted to see how she played everything out. I knew I had done nothing wrong, and I'm pretty sure the lawyer realized that as well. I told my principal that my last email laid out my stance and said I looked forward to the lawyer's response. Sadly, I didn't see her next move until it came. She wrote, "I don't feel any additional conversations would be productive at this point." That was like the little kid flipping the board because he was going to lose at Candyland. Like a lot of lawyers, she cared more about the money than about doing what was right by someone who wasn't her client.

The final result was that the administration of the medical practice refused to look me in the eye. They decided to think about money when they should have thought about my well-being. Doctors' offices are meant to help people, but they turned me away and did so in a fashion that was both disrespectful and completely lacking in empathy. Such is my life.

As a result of this episode in my life, I was left with the belief that the people who manage and run doctor's offices care more about themselves than those they serve. This medical practice's lack of care and response over the course of the year after Denise died contributed to this conviction, but the lawyer's letter poured gasoline on it and lit the match. My friend Eileen had a better analogy. She said they injected my mental health issues with steroids, which is true. I tried really hard to think these people cared, but, when push came to shove, they showed me clearly that they didn't.

I told the OB/GYN's lawyer that every year I would continue to ask her for a meeting with the medical practice administrator because even now I don't want to think these offices are only about money. Since I was unable to contact the practice directly, communicating with the law office was the best I could do. So far those requests have not been granted. I may never receive satisfaction and may have to live the rest of my life with the unfortunate mindset of mistrust toward the medical profession. That demon of distrust and doubt will be with me every time I talk with a doctor because I will know their secret: as long as you are giving them money and not being perceived as trying to take money, you are worth their time. But if they have any perception, no matter how false, that you represent a challenge to their finances, you will be shut out.

By this point in my journey of healing from the grief and anger, my attitude has softened somewhat. I realize doctors have an incredibly hard job. When their data turns out to be wrong and loss of life occurs, those doctors no doubt feel for their patients or the spouses and family members of those patients. However, the care they might want to show is hindered by the bottom line. The almighty dollar drives businesses, and sometimes that gets in the way of a human response.

I feel that the lawyer's letter, the subsequent emails, and all the denied requests have hurt more than just me. I believe some of the doctors in that practice, including the female doctor who wrote the note to me, probably had a desire to help a soul as wounded as mine but were prevented by those bottom-line concerns. I wanted to thank her from the bottom of my heart and to show her how instrumental her letter was in providing some relief on my healing journey. I wrote about this in my first book, which I would have shared with her had it not been for the severity of the lawyer's letter.

When the book was published, I had a conversation with my therapist because I wanted to send a copy to the doctor. We agreed that I would write something and then read it to my therapist, and then she would tell me if I should send the letter. I first read the letter from the lawyer and then the one I wrote to the doctor.

My therapist, rightfully so, advised me not to send the letter to the doctor. The attorney's letter was crystal clear that I was not to have contact with any of the doctors in the practice. Despite the fact that neither my own actions nor behavior prompted the letter in the first place, I was the one to whom the warning was issued. As an act of kindness and appreciation toward this amazing doctor, I wanted to share what I wrote and didn't send.

I think this letter also reveals my growth and the softening of my feelings toward the medical community. And, frankly, the grace she showed me deserves to be acknowledged. I wrote an initial note by hand followed by a second typed letter. The idea was that if she saw my name and didn't want to read the following pages, there would be no harm in that.

Initial Note:

10-22-20

Dear (female doctor's name),

First, let me assure you that I wish you no harm. I fully understand that my writing to you may make you feel uneasy. I only wish to let you know that the letter you wrote to me three years ago greatly improved my mental and emotional state. However, based on a letter I received last year, I have been warned about reaching out. I fully respect you and your boundaries, and, please, believe me when I state that I only wish to thank you for the letter you wrote. Out of concern that hearing from me might increase your anxiety, I wanted to write this note first. If you decide to throw this letter and envelope away, please do so. I will continue my writing on the next page if and only if you want to keep reading.
—Levi Moore

Letter That Followed:

Three years ago you sat in a room with me and (the male doctor's name) and helped me heal much more than you will ever understand. After I left your office, I had lunch with a co-worker who even saw how much better I was. I think one of the best things for me was getting in a room with you two and crying on (the male doctor)'s shoulder. You both showed me the compassion and care I needed for so long. I hated why we were there, but I was so grateful that you two were there for me.

After the meeting I wrote you both a thank-you note because you deserved it for showing me that you do care for me and my situation. I never in a million years expected to hear back from you. Your letter had a truly profound effect on my well-being. That meeting was the only time you or anyone affiliated with your organization reached out to me. The practice was always reactive to my requests, but that meeting and that letter were proactive. It made me feel you cared about me and that you could think with your heart and not your wallet. You will probably never write a letter that means more than that one. I doubt I will ever get one that means more to me than that letter.

I never responded because I didn't want you to feel bad or make you sad, especially after the compassion you showed me. However, I always felt I needed to thank you in some way. The only way I thought I could was to show you how much your letter helped me. I don't know if you remember when I met you two, but I said I was writing a book and the medical piece didn't look good. However, the two chapters I wrote about our meeting and your letter have been instrumental in my healing, and I felt the only way to thank you properly was to show you how much better my life was after you helped me.

My book is raw, real, and very hard. But that's how it should be. It's currently on Amazon. It's titled Nightmares Can Come True. I wouldn't recommend reading the medical chapter, but chapters 17 and 18 are my reflections about how you significantly helped me heal. The first book I received went to Denise, and the second book went to my initial grief counselor. The person who has had the greatest positive impact after those two is you. I know this tragedy was the reason for our meeting, but I will always be most thankful for the light in the darkness you offered. Your words forever changed me and quite possibly my outlook on doctors. Letting you know how much you helped me seemed to be the only true way to thank you for what you did. I do sincerely apologize if I upset you; that is not my intention.

If you were to let me send you a copy to properly thank you for your caring nature, I would be honored to let you know how much better my life has been since I received that letter.

—Levi Moore

The inner demon of anger still tells me doctors don't care and that their actions prove it. I don't want to believe that. But that shadow continues to have a say because of how this situation was mishandled.

As dedicated as I have been to seeking solutions and help for my ongoing depression, it continues to be there. I don't even know what I would say if I sat down with the administrator of that medical practice. I would want to look them in the eye and let them know they failed Denise and failed me by refusing to confront my pain and offer some solace. As painful as my world was in those days, I shouldn't have had to be the one seeking their kindness when they could have reached out to me and showed they cared about my survival, my healing, and my health.

We all fail when we think with our wallets instead of our hearts. Maybe that is how business is done these days. I can't help but wonder how they would have handled themselves if I'd ended my life. The world is full of people who don't care, but when the people who don't care are the ones we rely on for care, we are all losers.

Chapter 14

Family

The second biggest hurdle I had to deal with following the passing of Denise, Addison, and Lucas was navigating the evolving family dynamics. I am an only child, and my parents are retired and living in Tennessee. After meeting Denise, I moved to a place that was close to her sister, one of her best friends, and later her parents.

I truly loved being so close and a part of Denise's family. We spent many Saturday evenings playing cards and eating dinner with her parents. They were a short walk from our old house as well as our new home. Denise's family treated me as one of their own, and I felt part of something wonderful.

Since Denise and I were both schoolteachers and much of our extra funds were set side as we continued to pursue our goal of being parents, we often couldn't afford vacations. Thankfully, Denise's family was always great about letting us stay with them on trips. Apart from our honeymoon and one-year anniversary trip, we spent almost all our vacations with Denise's family.

Those were happy times when I felt like part of the family, and I hoped that would never change.

Sadly, when Denise passed away, we all faced incomprehensible circumstances that each of us had to find a way to navigate. The first week after Denise passed, amid shock and grief, we managed to perform like a well-oiled machine. Denise's sister and I were extremely close and made a lot of the decisions together. Her parents were instrumental in seeing us all through that time and were a part of every major decision as well. I even stayed at their house for a couple of weeks after Denise passed. It was a profound help that we could be supportive of each other in a time that seemed so bleak.

After a couple of weeks, I moved back into the house. My parents were there by this time and were kindly putting away some of the baby things so I didn't have to see them and feel overwhelmed with grief. While I wanted to continue to stay with Denise's parents, I understood that they, too, needed to grieve on their own without having to tend to my needs. Denise's passing brought us all together in a way and for a reason no one wanted to experience. We were proud we could still function together, but it was time for each of us to figure out how we could move forward individually after such a tragic loss.

Even after returning home, I continued to stay close to Denise's parents. After I went back to work, I still tried to go over and spend Friday evenings together. We would always get a pizza and then often watch a movie. It was pretty tricky for me to get groceries after work, take them home, put them away, and then rush over for dinner. Often, I was exhausted in the process, but we all wanted to maintain our strong sense of connection and to be supportive of each other, so I was determined to continue.

As time went on, we were each clearly struggling and sometimes we said things that weren't helpful. There were times when I left after our nights together feeling frustrated about some of their remarks, and I know there were occasions when I said something that was hurtful to them as well. Even so, we needed to spend time together both for mutual support and encouragement as well as to have someone with whom we could talk about Denise and how much we missed her. Because we were all suffering, there were plenty of unhelpful and unhealthy comments along the way. But my own road to healing was made more difficult because I always had to return to that empty house and live in an environment where Denise had taken her last breath. The reality was we were all confronting a situation that none of us knew how to face. The world took our precious Denise away, and we had to figure out how to heal.

I continued to put as many pieces of support in place as possible because I knew how incredibly hard my life was and would be in the future. I am forever thankful that I decided to actively seek support and professional help. I was making progress. It didn't seem so then, but my ability to talk through my experiences and issues was instrumental in my survival and growth. I wish we all would have gone to therapy. Nonetheless, I am glad I placed importance on getting the help I needed.

Another way I sought solace was through reading about grief during the first nine months after Denise's death. Many of the books discussed the fact that many families did not survive in such cases of extreme grief. I always believed that we as a family would make it through. We were close both in relationship and in proximity and often spent our vacations together. I felt Denise's family and I had all the characteristics needed to overcome something of this magnitude.

My conviction was so strong in this regard that I probably tried to stay around Denise's parents for longer than I should have. There were comments and pain on both sides, and the reality was that we weren't healthy for each other. I know they hated that I started to back away from them; it destroyed me inside as well, but it was something I had to do. Looking back, I wish I had been strong enough to pull away earlier; then maybe we wouldn't have been so hurtful to each other.

Denise's parents and I deeply love each other, yet we reached a point in our journey where being together no longer served our health and wellbeing. Once that occurred, retreating from one another was the right thing to do. One thing all those books on healing after a loss got right was that everyone grieves differently, which is why families often don't survive deaths as devastating as this one. I truly wish I had been stronger in those moments when our relationship started to falter. I wish I could have handled myself better for them. They didn't need to see me upset; they needed my support. I simply was dealing with too much pain and anger myself to offer the solace they required.

Grief is a balancing act. Sadly, our relationship was out of balance. In order to heal myself, I had to let go of a relationship that meant a great deal to me, but that prevented us all from finding our way past the pain.

There were still times when we could all get together and feel the old kinship and camaraderie. We took a couple of trips together that first year, but I think each of us was aware on some level that we were growing apart. Denise had created this bond, but it could no longer hold once she was gone and we had to withstand the crushing weight of profound loss.

At a certain point, I recognized that my presence in their lives was hurtful for the entire family. Even so, Denise's dad really tried to be supportive. He sent me a text every night and was truly concerned about how I was doing. There were times when he needed to care for his wife *and* for me, but he couldn't both at once. He handled that balancing act as well as he could. It took me far too long to realize how much my weakness weighed on him.

With Denise, I hadn't needed anything else. We hung out with her parents and sister a great deal of the time. I was completely fine with that. Denise was our connector who brought us together and kept us close. When she passed away, the family dynamics were irrevocably altered. That connection dissolved. Whether right or wrong, it doesn't matter. With her gone, we found it much harder to stay together. While she was alive, we shared countless moments of joy. After her death, our grief and understandable self-pity, our intense sense of loss, drove us into our own misery and apart from one another. Most families aren't going to come back from that kind of tragedy. It took me years to figure that out.

During that first year, I spent a fair amount of time around Denise's family; as the second year progressed, a little less so. At the time, I was too fragile to identify an issue that, looking back, I now see so clearly. Although Denise's family said nothing to me about this, it must have been insanely difficult to see me as often as they did, knowing that every time they were in my company they thought of Denise and ached with the pain of her absence!

In the midst of my loneliness and grief and in the type of depression that takes years to hopefully come out of, I wasn't able to recognize that truth. Looking back on that first year when we were together at Christmas, on the visit to Disney, and on a trip at Mother's Day, I realize now how brutally tough it must have been for them to escape their pain and have some fun with me there as a constant reminder.

I was so alone and in desperate need of support that I forced myself upon these people and never realized how much I probably hindered their healing. I know they all wanted to help and support me, but I never really looked at it from their shoes. I never saw it through their eyes. Seeing me reminded them relentlessly of the fact that they lost their daughter and their grandchildren.

While Denise was alive, I did not see the big picture of how I put myself in a box by not developing my own set of friends in the area. She was all I ever wanted and needed, so I failed to form the kinds of connections I needed outside of the family. On the one hand, this all-encompassing dedication to Denise made me a good husband. But because I let my world revolve around Denise, I lacked the outside friendships that might have supported my healing journey and would have allowed me to lean on someone who wasn't already carrying the burden of their own grief.

During those first couple of years, my loneliness grew more intense. I would teach and handle life at school well but then come home and not really hear from people. I wouldn't wish that type of life on anyone. I understood that no one knew what to say to someone like me. I spent the holidays with Denise's family only to return to an empty house and then not hear much from her sister. That was really tough on me. I came to realize that, during such times, we all end up looking after the people in our own house, and for me there was no one else at home.

Even my close friends struggled to figure out how to talk to me. Many of them weren't able to leave their families and drive a couple of hours to help me because they had busy lives. It left me in a really tough position.

I'm sure that we all think that things can't get much worse. After Denise passed, I started to question that. I was informed one day about a rumor that someone in the community made. Apparently, a former acquaintance thought she would make herself feel more important by sharing something false and cruel.

Shortly after Denise passed, I worried that she might have been screaming for my help and I wasn't there for her. After I woke up that morning, I put in my earbuds to do some housework before

Denise got up. Later, the horrible thought came to me that she might have been calling out to me and I couldn't hear her. That thought was soon put to rest when we were told that Denise died instantly and without any pain.

This individual somehow heard about my brief but dreadful fear that Denise needed me when she was dying and I wasn't there, and decided to go to her hairdresser and tell them that my wife was dying and crying out to me, and I was ignoring her. This world seems to be full of absolutely terrible people. Well, when I heard about this, I needed to talk to her and tell her what a horrible thing that was. A couple of days passed before I had an opportunity to speak with her. Needless to say, I didn't sleep through the night until we connected because of my anger.

When we talked, she didn't take responsibility for her actions and tried to weasel her way out of this mistake. I was fuming during the conversation as a result. I finally just said, "Can we both agree that you said something you shouldn't have?" She agreed and that was the end. She did tell me who told her this misinformation. Shortly thereafter, the person called and informed me that this is not what they said. Either way, she was in the wrong. I will always remember how she treats people who need care and comfort. She spreads lies to make herself feel important.

Like a lot of people in the world, this absolutely despicable individual had a better life than I had during those excruciating days. It seemed that pretty much everyone I knew had enviable lives. My feelings of jealousy and anger at other people hurt many of the relationships I had with Denise's additional family members.

I was lucky enough to have one of the speakers at Denise's funeral and her husband, who was a pallbearer, come over to sit with me regularly for about six months. Having someone other than my parents inside the house meant everything to me during those first six months. I was so empty and alone and needed every support possible. I will always thank those two for visiting me. They had loved Denise, and I thought they loved me too, but after six months I didn't hear from them at all.

The other speaker at Denise's funeral and her husband, who also was a pallbearer, lived in California. In this day and age of text messaging, email, and cell phones, I had hoped we would have a conversation of some description at least. Sadly, that never happened, which fed my feelings about being cut off from the world.

There were a number of people who never reached out to me, which increased my sense of isolation and lack of support. I believe anyone in my shoes would have wanted others to show up and be there. But a part of me understood that, for her friends and family to think of me, they would have to think about Denise, and, frankly, because of the tragic nature of her death, for their own mental health, moving on and remaining at a distance from me may have been the only way they could function.

When I spoke with a couple of Denise's friends and with her sister, it didn't really change anything. They were aware I was in pain; they didn't have to visit me to know that, but I wanted to see them to let them know I really needed them. However, that wasn't going to happen. The writing was on the wall. I didn't force myself on these people. I respected their need for space and time but wished they had shown me the love and compassion I sought. I will always look back on those first two years after Denise's passing as truly awful.

When I spoke to people from Denise's life, they were thoughtful and caring, but the fact remained that I always returned to an empty home and a lonely, shattered life.

We all grieve differently. I suspect they all felt this tragedy was so horrific that the only way they could continue to function was to just keep going. If they became too involved with me, I may well have brought them down into my hole of despair. I was still leaning deeply into the grief and edging too close to the abyss for them to provide me the support I needed.

I was afraid that if I lost Denise's family and friends, I would lose part of her. That's why I tried as hard as I could to be with them. I didn't know quite how to handle this fear.

After the second year, I knew I needed to change my headspace. During the first year, I worked hard to remain "nice" when I spoke with everyone, but I needed to voice my deeper truth after that, even if it meant people didn't want to see me again.

I met with Denise's best friend and husband who had spent time with me for six months. They came over, and I really was honest with them. They knew they had let me down, but they had their own lives to live and had family members of their own who were in the hospital, so they weren't able to be there for me. Looking back on our conversation from a few years out, I realize how meaningful it was. They were as honest as I was, and some of what they said was tough for me to hear. It was difficult for me to realize that I wasn't the only one dealing with issues. Unfortunately, at the time, instead of seeing their honesty as a mark of compassion, I viewed their words as a comparison between what I was going through and their own situation. I assume that's why they say you should never compare grief. In my depressed state, it was impossible not to compare what I was going through to others.

Denise's family and I continued to have a difficult time. At one point my father-in-law said something that was hard for me to hear. He was driving me home from their house one night and said, "I think this has been as hard on (Denise's mother) as it's been on you."

I almost blew up at him but instead let the comment stand. As horrible as it was for them, they at least had each other. They were not alone in their grief as I was after losing my wife, our full-term twins, and the future we had envisioned for our lives.

The fact that I said nothing in response opened the way for this painful remark to be repeated later. The second time my father-in-law made this statement, I yelled that I didn't think he had any idea how hard it was to live in that house by myself. He tried to apologize and I know he felt bad. He didn't mean to upset me; he was just trying to let me know I wasn't the only one experiencing devastating pain.

I believe Denise's sister struggled a lot more than I ever realized. I held a lot of frustration that I didn't hear much from her. There were too few conversations asking how I was holding up. I think she needed just to maintain her life as a mother, wife, daughter, and employee to stay sane through such loss. Those first two years stranded in my house alone, I felt the harsh reality of my own situation and couldn't help comparing my life to those who had a family to grieve with them.

During a long run on a Saturday morning, I realized it was time to change my mindset and try to better deal with the tragedy that happened two years earlier. I knew I needed to talk to Denise's sister and also to figure out how I could surround myself with people who would support my journey in this cruel world.

Chapter 15

Friends

As Thanksgiving approached, two years after Denise's passing, the first thing I did to change my mindset was what I refer to as the "Thankfulness Tour." As much as I longed for connection and felt isolated, there were people who did reach out. They simply weren't as close in proximity as I wished. A really great friend with whom I hadn't spoken in about 15 years contacted me after Denise passed away.

When I was in high school, I met a wonderful, fun family named the Kents. I worked with their three oldest sisters and then their brother. We always got along really well. After I graduated from college and moved to North Carolina, I lost contact with them. But when Denise died, they rose to the occasion.

I received letters from a couple of the Kent girls and one from their brother Jeff. I always wrote back because anyone who was willing to make the effort to contact me in my circumstances deserved a handwritten letter in return. In the years since, Jeff and I have continued to correspond. After a while, we began using the computer to type our letters for the sake of time. But those handwritten letters from Jeff at the bleakest time in my life meant everything to me. I really enjoyed hearing what he and his family were doing, but, most meaningfully, I was grateful that he asked how I was actually feeling.

Jeff hadn't seen me in years before this tragedy, but he figured out a way to reach out and build rapport with me. This kind of commitment to caring about someone who is suffering profound grief is a testament to the kind of person Jeff is and something others would do well to emulate in similar situations.

Jeff and I became very close through our monthly letters, and he was probably the first person who came to mind when I thought about changing my outlook. I wrote that I was thinking of getting out of North Carolina for the Thanksgiving break and wanted to know if I could visit him and essentially crash his holiday. I had no idea what he would be doing, but I figured the worst answer I could get was a no. (This was before I received the lawyer's response that I was essentially mentally ill.) Sure enough, Jeff said that he was actually hosting the family's Thanksgiving dinner and would be delighted if I came and crashed their party.

Thanksgiving morning, I stopped by Denise's niche at the columbarium and then visited her school bench before heading out on my almost eight-hour solo drive. Leaving the state felt like letting out a deep sigh. My thought patterns at that time definitely needed adjusting, and seeing Jeff and his family was an extremely welcome treat.

I stopped by my old house where I had lived in Ohio and took a couple of photos since I had no idea when I would be in Ohio again. Then, I drove to Jeff's to visit people I hadn't seen in years. I felt weird after arriving. Here I was about to enter a family occasion carrying the weight of my tragic circumstances. Had I been among those attendees at Thanksgiving hearing about my visit after 15 years, I might well have said, "And we think this is a good idea?"

The Kents were a large family, and sometimes it was difficult to get a response from everyone. However, Jeff told me later that, when he asked if it would be okay if I attended, he received a quick and unanimous "yes" from everyone. At least that's what I was told, and I believe it because when I arrived they were all so welcoming.

Walking into a place with people you haven't seen for so many years might well feel strange, but they were all so openhearted and friendly. They seemed to have aged very little in those years, and their kindness was just as it once had been.

I hung out with their family that evening and for a couple of additional days before I left to headed up to Cleveland to see another friend on my Thankfulness Tour. The Kents showed me the compassion I needed during that intensely sad period. I will forever be grateful to the entire Kent family for how they treated me.

Next, I visited Val, a friend from college. Val and I were really good friends in college as we were both finishing our teaching degrees. Val was super cool and popular, and I wasn't either, but we became close anyway. My popularity and street credit increased as a result of hanging out with Val. We attended a number of concerts together, and she used to come and stay with my family and me afterward. My parents knew her as "Hot Val" because I had told them how beautiful she was. Until they saw her, I don't think either of my parents ever realized how cool their son was for hanging out with someone as amazing as Val.

Val was another one of those people who continued to reach out and talk to me during those first couple of years after Denise's passing. Val was really sweet and caring. When I approached her about a visit, she was genuinely excited to see me. I was equally delighted to meet her husband and two daughters. We had a wonderful time seeing the sights of Cleveland and just spending time together. I did some pretty impressive coloring with their two girls. Being around this loving family was far healthier for me than feeling isolated at home.

After a couple of days with Val and her family, I headed back to Columbus to see my friend Tim. He was a really great friend and boss. I worked with and for Tim in an educational program at the Columbus Zoo. He was the best man at my wedding and even took a trip down to stay with me for a weekend that first year after Denise passed. He was always caring and kind and able to make me laugh even during difficult times.

During my visit, we went to the zoo one day. All the people there who knew me were shocked by my visit and clearly had no idea what to say to me. It felt odd. I realized I would probably never see those people again, but it simply was what it was.

After a couple of days with Tim and his family, it was time to return to North Carolina and into the heart of my depression.

That trip really did a great deal for my mental state at that time. I was so sad, angry, and jealous of the lives of those around me. My feelings were compounded by the fact that people had no idea what to say or how to act around me.

Jeff Kent
Friend/Former Coworker

Why did I reach out/write a letter? *We were at Thanksgiving with my family in Nashville one year (I think it was 2016), and Aileen filled me in on the news. I really hadn't ever experienced a friend going through such a personal tragedy before. Friends from high school had lost parents to cancer, but Levi's experience was so extreme. We had been friends for so long, and, while we hadn't kept in touch for many years, I think we all felt like family from working together for so many summers. Working at the Columbus Zoo was so good in so many ways, and I always reflect fondly on my friendships from those summers. I made friends with people older and younger than me, from different parts of town and different schools, with different life aspirations. But none of that mattered. We were bonded in friendship by working together and a lot of times by hanging out together after work.*

When I heard about what had happened, my heart splintered, and it weighed on me for so many days. I had to reach out. I did not know how to help. I did not want to be intrusive because we had lost touch. I felt a written letter would let Levi know I was sincere in my condolences and that I wanted to help. I also felt it would be easy for him to let go if he wasn't ready to rebuild an old relationship.

Why did I keep writing? *I felt committed to keeping in communication because I wanted Levi to know it was not just a whim that I reached out in the first place. Levi's journey to healing, however long and* *difficult, was something I wanted to be a part of in any way possible. Had I stopped writing, I feel like I would have failed as a friend.*

Thanksgiving visit – *When I invited Levi to Thanksgiving, I really wondered what my wife, Anissa, would think. She had never met him. We had an eight-month-old, and Anissa was six months pregnant. So many questions went through my mind. What if Levi isn't the same person I remember? What will my wife think if he is the same weird person I remember?! Will it be painful for him to see lots of little kids, and will he get sad seeing my wife is pregnant? I honestly never worried about the rest of my family. I knew they would be so happy to have him with us.*

I'm so glad Levi came; it was such a special holiday. My wife and I look back on that weekend with such joy and are so glad we could have him in our home.

All other stuff – *One of the things I like most about continuing to write to Levi on a regular basis is that it helps me reflect on life in a deeper way. I pause to think about what has happened and what the most important stuff to share is. Going through that thinking process really helps put perspective on life for me. I also really love seeing how Levi's life is changing. I can imagine how difficult it is some days, but I'll never know. Getting a glimpse into the grieving and some of the healing has actually been a blessing, especially with my Dad's passing two years ago. I used to tell my friends and my wife a few years ago that I knew I was doomed for an apocalypse because my life was so* *blessed and I had never really experienced a major tragedy or loss. And now that I've experienced some very painful losses, I think I can draw from some of your emotions and processing. No loss is the same, and I'm still incredibly lucky. But dealing with my losses has definitely been more doable because of our relationship.*

In good times or bad, it's always nice to reconnect with an old friend. You know you're good friends when you can disappear for years but then pick up right where you left off when you do reconnect. Outside of the circumstances that brought us together, it's great to reconnect with an old friend who knows and understands me.

After returning to North Carolina, I was able to hold myself together until Christmas. When I went to see my parents, however, I still held a lot of anger inside. I had asked to meet with Denise's sister in early November, and after that she appeared to be avoiding me. It took a lot for me to actually ask to have a talk; I knew it wouldn't be easy but, to be fair, there wasn't much about my life that was easy then. However, I never heard from her. She knew I wanted to talk to her. I was understanding enough to wait until after her birthday to broach the subject, but sadly it seemed I was left with my hand out.

I was in such terrible shape during that time that my parents realized they couldn't even mention her name around me that Christmas. I hated that version of myself, but I was actively trying to make myself better. My efforts weren't working, though, because the person I needed to talk to about these issues was avoiding me. When your mental state depends on people you can't depend on, your feelings often deteriorate—a lesson I was learning the hard way.

Upon arriving home after the holiday break, I tried to schedule an appointment with my own doctor because I knew it was time to get some medication to ease my stress, anger, and depression. I needed to allow my thoughts and feelings to be expressed by having tough conversations, but people were avoiding me, which made my situation worse.

Again, I wish I could have been far more understanding and less selfish, that I could have recognized how hard it was for Denise's family to be around me, let alone have a difficult conversation with me. But during that time I was driven by sorrow, anger, jealously, and selfishness. I didn't perceive how difficult it would be for them. I only knew that I needed to have these conversations so I could sleep at night and let go of some of my feelings. My anger intensified when I didn't get what I wanted and felt I deserved.

Finally, I was able to reach her, and we got together to plan our upcoming Run for Dee Dee 5K. We found a time when I could sit down with her and her husband and we could have this talk I had needed for so long.

I'm sure that meeting was harder for them than it was for me. I lived every day in that depressive state for over two years. Most other people had no idea how bad off I was either because they didn't want to know or didn't try to find out. Denise's sister and her husband were both honest and open. That's what we all should have been in those years after Denise passed. I needed them to see me as I was in the depths of my pain, and it was healthier for me to recognize that they were still hurting too. We all took accountability for our actions.

One of my big issues was that some of our memorial fund checks were not getting written. The last thing I wanted was the world forgetting Denise. I felt if we didn't write our memorial fund checks then we were making it much easier for the world to forget about her. Denise's sister explained that she had gotten too busy with work and had let that responsibility slide more than she ever wanted. I was glad she seemed to show remorse. We three talked about how hard all of this was, and my brother-in-law said something that I will never forget.

He looked at me through his glasses and said, "We can't change the past, but we can do better."

He was right. To be fair, that worked both ways. I was always overly cautious about reaching out to either of them because I didn't want to inflict my darkness on their world. At the same time, I still needed them to understand how dark my world was.

After we talked, we all agreed to do better and put a couple of dates on our calendar to get together and have more fun like we used to. When those dates came, we did have fun. In fact, we always had an enjoyable time whenever we were in the same room. However, they had a life to live and a brilliant and compassionate daughter to raise; their main focus should be Sara, not me. Their attention should be directed toward giving her the best childhood possible. As much as it hurt me to miss them, I always admired how amazing they were as parents.

Although our relationship improved, I remember driving home after a couple of our evenings together and thinking that I probably wasn't going to hear much from them until the next visit, which made me sad. Our relationship grew after we had finally spoken and I was able to share my feelings, but I hadn't forgotten that Thanksgiving and Christmas when she had tried to avoid me. As much as I cared for and loved them, I clearly no longer felt like part of the family. Family supports and loves you through the most difficult times; they don't avoid you. Denise was the part of their family that they lost; I wasn't. I finally realized that. I came to understand that I needed to develop my own friendships, and Denise's family needed to keep moving forward rather than letting me drag them down into a place of constant pain. I will always love her family, but we needed to go our separate ways. I'm truly thankful they didn't let me anchor them in sorrow and pull them into my depression. Each of us had to discover our own path to healing.

Judy Halsey
Denise's Mother

Nightmares Really Do Come True was the perfect title for Levi's first grief book. Nightmares you never in a million years think would happen. Our lives were all changed in a moment.

On Saturday evening, October 22, 2016, we invited Levi and Denise and also Dawn and Sara (Denise's sister and niece) over for dinner. Brian was out of town. We had a nice evening and watched the playoff game that sent the Cubs to the World Series. When the game was about to end, Denise got very uncomfortable so she and Levi went home and watched the rest in bed. She was so excited that they won and were going to the series! She texted us, 'Cubs win, Cubs win.' Little did we ever know that would be our last hug goodbye that night and the last text we would ever get from her.

The next morning, Bill and I went to church, and I had left my phone in the car. When we got in the car, there was a message from Levi, so we thought Denise had gone into labor; however, unfortunately, that was not the case. We had lost her and the full-term babies. What an emotional rollercoaster!

We all came back to our home. Luckily, our pastors, Gene and Valerie, came over immediately to try to console us and pray with us. They were with us nearly every day from that day through the funeral. We were all upset, of course, with the doctors and with God. Why would God do such a thing to a family that has always tried to live up to our upbringing and our faith in God? Why? Why? Why? Like the pastors said, we may never know even when we are in heaven with her.

After Denise's funeral friends and family went on with their jobs and families. Being retired, Bill and I were just home by ourselves. As Levi stated, yes, we did have each other but didn't know what to do next. Levi was with us for a couple of weeks, and then he went back to teaching, which we told him, as hard as it would be, would be best for him. Dawn and Brian were home also for a week to try to go through some of the grieving process. Being only eight at the time, Sara was at a total loss and could not express her feelings of losing her Aunt DeDe as she called her. Denise was her hero and her only aunt.

We did experience family tension during the time after, but, as we were told in one of our grief meetings, there is no grief worse than another. We think Levi and our family would have not necessarily agreed. We have lost parents, grandparents, aunts, uncles, and cousins and very close friends. Luckily, most of them lived a fulfilled life and were in their later years. It was heartbreaking to lose each and every one of them; we loved them and we think about them all the time. Denise had many years of life to go on with Levi and her as parents to a beautiful set of twins who didn't even get to live.

We all went to a grief share class at our church in the following months. I felt it was helpful in some ways, but, no matter what you do, you can learn to deal with your grief, but the pain will always be in your heart. During grief share, one of the questions was if our friends had more of less abandoned us. I believe we were all in agreement that they had—not all of them, of course. The ones we had known for years were the ones who were staying away more than friends we had only known for a few years. We got so many calls with messages saying, 'Call when you want to talk about it!' That really was upsetting because I felt it was so they had the gossip. I hope I am wrong, and God forgive me for thinking that.

We were fortunate that we had the pastors (Valerie and Gene) during this time to counsel us when we needed it or just to call to say hi. We also had some home visits from a Compassionate Friends counselor. These are counselors who have lost a child, so they know what you are going through, and, of course, we had grief share. We learned not to ask, 'How are you?' to someone who has lost a loved one but rather to say, 'It is so good to see you,' and give them a little hug; that does wonders. No one would have wanted to hear our true answer as to how we are.

I know it has been tough for Levi, and we understand that he was left alone. We are so happy for him that he is moving on with his life as we are all trying to. Being the fun-loving person she always was and still is in heaven, Denise would have wanted Levi and the rest of us to move on. We do miss seeing you more often, Levi, and please know you will always be loved by our family.

> The only advice I can give to anyone who loses someone is to get counseling; it may even be provided by your church. You will question your faith as we did, but the only thing to do is rely on your Christian teachings and upbringing that there is a beautiful life to come in paradise and trust that your loved ones are in Jesus' loving arms and you will all meet again.
>
> I would like to close with this verse that Pastor Valerie read when Denise was at her final resting place.

Sleep on, Beloved.

Sleep and take thy rest.

Lay down your weary head

Upon thy Savior's breast.

We love thee well,
But Jesus loves thee best.
—Author Unknown

As I attempted to regain more balance in my life, I took Facebook off my phone, kept my cell in the other room, and sought positive friendships with people who were healthy. Most people my age had families and busy lives and weren't able to drop everything to spend time with me. How could people juggle active family lives and friendships?

But I found some friends who could be there during those trying times. My buddy Rick Williams, who is married to Denise's cousin, visited, and we played chess and met for a couple of dinners. My former student teacher also had me over on a number of occasions. During one of my favorite evenings, I told her and her husband to come up with as many difficult questions as they could and said I would answer every one of them. People didn't know how to talk to me in those days and were afraid to bring up painful subjects. What they didn't realize was that I asked myself every tough question in my countless hours alone. That's what I needed to do. It was great to get their perspective on my life.

I had the wonderful fortune of meeting a family I continue to see and love. When the Gardiniers initially donated to the 5K race, I didn't even know them. After their donation, I asked if I could drop off some T-shirts from the race for them, and they invited me to dinner. We had an incredible meal, and I enjoyed spending time with them and their two delightful daughters. We played some competitive Apples to Apples, and then they asked me how I was doing.

After meeting the Gardiniers, my dad got one of those few happy phone calls from me. Dad was so often the recipient of heartbreaking calls from me, so I wanted to even out the negative with more of the positive. Even now, when I call him, I always begin, "This is a good call."

I met with my friend Jared, who looked over my book, and I got to have dinners with another great family, the Royers. Melissa Royer had worked with Denise, and Thomas worked in law for the state. They were always supportive. When I spent time around them, I didn't have to pretend that my life was great. I could just enjoy them and their compassion and kindness. Thomas and I went to some NC State basketball games, and the family and I attended the opening of a new minor league baseball stadium.

I was steadily improving my outlook but found that shifting into a new life can be uncomfortable. This transition needed to happen despite the discomfort. Although I was still filled with sadness when I was alone in the house, these outings and time spent among friends were good for me.

Many people still had no idea how to talk to me, of course. When I saw those from my former life, the sense of unease remained, but I had become much better at handling myself and my situation.

Running with my friend Eileen and being part of the relay team lifted my spirits and enhanced my mental health. As time passed, people at school became more involved in my life. It took about three and a half years for me to feel comfortable with my life. My life was far from perfect, but I gradually felt more at ease in my own skin. I was open to talk honestly about all that had happened, which I believe made people around me better able to discuss where I was on the journey.

At my age, I'm not out meeting many new people, so those I'm close to tend to be my colleagues. Since early education and elementary schools are populated primarily by women, many of my good friends were and are females. I always felt that women were more compassionate, so being in that environment probably helped immensely. I was able to laugh more and put on fun little events for friends. I was so proud when I started watching my friend's dogs. Since I always feel gratified about filling a weekend without spending any money, I consistently offered to watch my friend's dogs. That was a really cheap way to occupy my time and help friends who had done such a great job of supporting me.

Some issues with Denise's family remained and probably will always be there. When I was invited to a birthday party for Denise's sister, I said the reason I wouldn't attend was that I didn't feel like part of the family. I knew that would be hard to hear, but it was honest. Looking back, I really wish I hadn't said that because it was hurtful. At the same time, I needed the family to know where I was. Sadly, the response I received was a text message that clearly wasn't intended for me. Again, I felt there was a lack of accountability on their part, which showed an unwillingness to change. The text message and the subsequent phone call pretty much spelled the end of my involvement with Denise's family, which was a shame. We all try to do what we can in such situations, and what is good for one person isn't necessarily beneficial for everyone.

Overall, I've been able to make progress and feel comfortable with the people in my life now. One day, on my way to therapy, I dropped by the funeral home and spoke with Grant, the man who helped with the viewing and funeral and was such a caring soul during that first terrible week. He is of a high-class character. I think the gratitude I expressed on that visit meant a lot to him. Thanking those who are kind to me will always be important on my journey through life.

After five years, I feel grateful for the friends in my life. I'm lucky they helped me get to where I am today, and I hope to continue to let them know how much their friendship matters.

Since I am at a much better place, I continue to check in on my little niece Sara. She has two wonderful, loving, and supportive parents and is really a wonderful kid. I think she is going to grow into a truly special person. One day, she invited me to her dance recital. I knew it would be interesting with all the family being there, but I wanted to be there for Sara. If my niece wanted me there, well, that was where I was going to be.

The weekend of the dance recital turned out to be when we experienced a severe gas shortage. That Friday before the recital, my district actually canceled school because of the transportation and gas issue. I really wanted to go but was concerned about my limited gas, which I felt I needed to save for trips to and from work. Sara was rightfully disappointed when I explained that I couldn't attend after all.

That's when my brother-in-law stepped in and stepped up. He reached out to me to see if the gas shortage was the real reason I decided not to attend or if I was really using that as an excuse. When I said the gas shortage was truly the reason, he offered to pick me up in his electric car. It was great to see him and catch up. As much frustration as the family and I have experienced in our relationship, I consider him a really great guy and know he does truly care.

I was happy that I got to be there for Sara's dance recital. I saw a couple of people I knew through Denise; some acknowledged me while others didn't, which was fine. I wasn't there for anyone else other than Sara. I talked with Denise's parents and sister, and we all went to dinner together after the recital. What a beautiful moment! We all had put each other through the ringer, but the fact that we could all come together for Sara spoke volumes about each and every one of us. Although there was some tension and probably always will be, the day was a success. It was good to see them all and I'm glad they were happy to see me. We didn't talk much after that and, honestly, we didn't need to.

Denise brought us together and, when she died, it was never going to be the same. It took us (mostly me) much longer to realize that than it should have. My inability to realize it sooner probably hindered our relationship. We never really shared many common interests. The one thing we shared was Denise. With her gone, we couldn't find a way to return to the happy family we had once been before tragedy struck our lives. All of us coming together for Sara was the best ending to our shared journey.

I will always know that I screwed up. I was so nearsighted in the midst of my grief. I couldn't see the clear issue in the front of everyone's minds. Every time any of them saw me, they experienced again the loss of Denise, which, frankly, had to be absolute torture. While I was the one left to live in that house and in my utter loneliness, they had their own grief, which was powerful too. Denise, who had served as a bridge to her family and friends, was no longer there. I became an island surrounded by a vast ocean with no means of connecting. But that was the way it had to be. Maybe if I'd been more mature, more insightful, I could have stopped trying to traverse that ocean and saved everyone the tension we dealt with for so long. The crazy thing is that I know we all still love each other. Each of us loved Denise so much that we will always care for one another because she would want us to.

I recall my painful reactions to things people did and said, but I now understand that each of us was suffering so much that we weren't able to navigate each other's feelings thoughtfully. We were in survival mode, just trying to live through the worst experience of our lives. We did that. I was so weak and broken by Denise's death. I can only hope I didn't entirely destroy my relationships with the people Denise loved so dearly.

Chapter 16

Coronavirus

While I continued to grow and make improvements in my day-to-day life, the world was about to change dramatically. It took me three and a half years to find my calm and restore my equilibrium. Just as I was returning to a healthier frame of mind, everything we once knew was altered beyond imagining.

I remember opening Twitter one morning and reading that an NBA basketball game had been postponed because one of the players tested positive for COVID-19. Around the same time, Tom Hanks tested positive as well. During one of our Thursday morning meetings, I recall talking with one of my coworkers about how crazy the NBA shutdown was. The rest of that day, I went on about my work as usual. After school, I went to see a wonderful woman named Kami whom I had met six months earlier. She and I both experienced the heartbreaking loss of a spouse while in our thirties. As Kami and I shared an evening together, we both knew that something was going on, but it hadn't yet reached our doorstep.

We ate dinner outside at some restaurant and enjoyed catching up after not seeing each other for about a month. After dinner, we got into her vehicle and drove to a place nearby where a widow's panel was being held. I had never been to one and was fortunate that Kami recommended attending and was willing to go with me. Upon entering, we had to sign a piece of paper stating that we didn't have any flu-like symptoms and then use the available hand sanitizer.

We found seats in the back. Apart from one lady who appeared to be on the eight-person widow panel, we were clearly two of the three youngest people there. Being there with Kami was really good. We listened to the widows on the panel discuss various conflicts and challenges they had experienced. I thought the evening was beneficial. Kami noticed the guy sitting next to her was having a hard time. At the conclusion of the panel, we started to talk to him. His name was Greg, and he had just lost his wife within the last few months. He clearly was struggling as anyone in his situation would be.

Kami and I told him what brought us to the panel, and he seemed to appreciate us sharing our stories. We did our best to help him. It always feels good to support others, and we were grateful to be there for Greg.

After Kami dropped me off at my car, I started to drive the 45 minutes home. I had mentioned to dad previously that I might call him on the way home since there wouldn't be much traffic, and it would be good to catch up.

While talking to dad, he mentioned the virus and said he wasn't sure if he and mom would be able to make it to our Run for Dee Dee 5K this year. The race was in less than a month, and

Living through my Nightmare

I remember telling him I didn't think it would be wise for them to come either. My father volunteers at an assisted living facility, so he is always so much more cautious about the places he goes because he knows that he has responsibilities even in his retirement.

All things considered, I felt it was best for my parents not to come over. I even mentioned that there was a chance we might not even have the race. If things continued the way they were going, getting people together, even outside, wasn't a smart move. Also, knowing that people's health was at stake, it seemed irresponsible to push forward if things continued to progress as they had been.

We left it at that. As I arrived home, I reminded dad how nice it was to be able to talk to him without crying and feeling like I was dropping all my sadness and sorrow on him. My dad wouldn't admit it because he is a wonderful father, but I know he hated being on the wrong end of those phone calls over the previous years.

The next day at school was Friday the 13th, and I asked a couple of people at school if they felt weird about being there. Some of them felt the same way I did. Something was going on, and I believe another neighboring school district took the day off because they saw what was approaching.

At the end of school, we all grabbed our school bags and most everything we could carry, including our school computers, because we had no idea what would happen come Monday morning.

The next morning, I took one of my long runs with my friend Meredith. She worked in the medical field and understood the seriousness of what was happening. After the run, Meredith saw in the news on her phone that my school district commented that their policy on absences was going to be more lenient because of the virus. I remember telling Meredith, "That's a half step. The other shoe is going to drop."

Sure enough, later that day, a school employee close to where I lived tested positive, and the state put schools on hold. It was the right move, but it still seemed to happen so quickly. I really didn't know what to do or say. We were about to figure out how well I could function without the support and structure the school provided.

I got relatively lucky in that I was able to pick up the order for our 5K race shirts during that first week, so I stayed somewhat busy while the school district tried to figure out how we were going to handle the pandemic. I laid out all the race T-shirts, folded them, and placed them in the downstairs bedrooms. Next, I put all the running bibs and safety pins together and then added them to the T-shirts. It took quite a bit of time.

Usually, I organized all the materials during the weekend, and then Denise's parents came over to stuff the race packets. However, this year I was able to do it all while being at home.

Coronavirus essentially stopped school, church, and every other means of support I had put in place to cope with loss and grief. If the pandemic had happened a year or two earlier, I would have been in a much more precarious situation because I wasn't in the headspace then to survive being in that house alone on an ongoing basis.

As that first week progressed, it became clear we would not have our race. As much as the race represents a good cause, it isn't worth people's health. I emailed everyone to let them know I had their T-shirt, race bib, medal, and prize and would be happy to give them out at my house or meet them at a neighboring park on a weekend. When those times came, I sat outside and passed out as many as I could. Most people picked up their packets and some didn't. Everyone had paid already, but I only had one person demand a full refund. I was able to take care of that quickly. I was grateful for something to draw my focus and keep me busy.

The next week, the school district still wasn't offering much guidance about how we would move forward, but we had done some virtual meetings. Since I knew how to set those up, I reached out to a couple of the parents who were helpful at organizing, and we put in place a couple of tutoring or check-in sessions with my students. I think the parents appreciated hearing from me since everyone was still scrambling to figure out our new normal.

All things considered, I was actually coping incredibly well at home. I have always been a really organized individual, so when this happened and I lost the school and church structure, I was able to adapt pretty well because I was already self-disciplined.

It was still lonely beyond belief in the house, and not talking to anyone was tough, but I handled it much better than most people. I found myself getting into some solid routines.

I set my alarm early each morning and read for about 30 minutes before getting up, eating a banana, and exercising. I either ran around the neighborhood or used the elliptical, then showered and read some more. I went back and forth between reading and staring into my computer, either waiting for information from the county or hosting one of my tutoring sessions. At a certain point, I was having a number of morning meetings, but I just moved right from those back to my book until about 4:00 p.m. when I had a little snack and then went for a walk. As we got into summer, I often had to come back after my walk and take a shower. After that, I usually ate dinner, relaxed, and read again before going to sleep.

I did this routine daily—even on weekends. Many Saturday mornings, I went for a long run, showered, and then picked up a book and read, alternating between my book and house chores. I also talked with my dad and told him how I was doing. I think we were both shocked at how well I was holding up during those months of pandemic forced solitude.

I was pretty adamant about not turning on the TV during the school day. I felt immense guilt about so many people losing their jobs and deeply saddened by the pandemic's death toll. The idea of sitting around watching TV during the school day felt wrong. By reading, I was doing something more educational. I reached a point when I was reading about 100 pages a day and finishing books within a couple of days. Three years earlier, I had filled my time constructing LEGO Architecture sets. Now, I was ordering and reading books.

I really tried to exercise my brain regularly. It would have been all too easy to get into routines that held my focus but did nothing to feed my intellect. Instead, I chose to better myself during those countless hours of alone time.

One disappointment during those days was that my friend Lindsay, who had devoted a lot of time to training for a fast marathon, was unable to run it because they canceled the race. She had worked months before school each day, hoping to achieve a personal record. I never had a shot at reaching the goal she was aiming for, but, after seeing the times on some of her runs, I knew she could do it. She never got the chance because of the pandemic.

Because the race was canceled, my friends Meredith, Eileen, Kayla, and I decided to put on a fun race for Lindsay. The five of us enjoyed doing that little celebration event for Lindsay so much that we wanted to plan a few more similar occasions. We held a few small outdoor running and socializing events that were positive and fun. I was lucky to have good friends in my corner during this time in the world.

On the surface I seemed like someone who would have struggled tremendously during the pandemic, but I had been so structured and determined to heal and grow that, when the world came to a standstill, amazingly I was able to handle being alone for months. I realized how much better I was than even I had thought. The way I handled my alone time showed how far I had progressed. I was extremely proud of how far I had come on my healing journey and ever grateful that the world didn't stop a year or two earlier.

I had reached a point when I knew I would be able to move when the time came to leave that house. Many people asked me early on about why I continued to remain in the house where Denise had died. I would try to articulate to them that I believed I would have felt a great deal of guilt about leaving in those early days. It would have felt like closing a chapter of my life far too early. However, seeing the progress I had made while being forced to remain alone for the most part proved that I could move without feeling remorseful. I now knew that I was strong enough to find my way to a new life when the time was right and understood that Denise would always be in my heart wherever I was.

Chapter 17

The House

Every part of that house belonged to Denise. When we decided to build a new home and put our existing place on the market, Denise was the driving force behind that. We talked about the layout and design, of course, but everything inside and outside of the home we built was touched by her style and her presence.

    I still remember the Saturday that Denise and I met with our realtor and walked through the designer showroom to pick out countertops, backsplash, hardwoods, and everything else for the house we were building. Denise was looking at a couple of things in the first section, and then she said, "I need to see this," and we had to move to the second section to figure out the answers to her questions about the first section. I just looked at our realtor and we both laughed. We knew then that we were in for a long day.

    When we finally moved into the house, Denise picked a great set of colors for the outside and spent a lot of time making decisions for the inside. Ours was a beautiful house that we looked forward to living in for years with our kids. Of course, that wasn't the way our story ended. I had to live in that house alone after Denise left this world. That home had everything one could want in terms of comfort, beauty, and warmth, but it was a cold, bitterly lonely place without her.

After Denise passed, my family and I had a difficult discussion about work. My principal was truly kind and understanding about transitioning me gently back into my job after Denise passed. But my parents and I weren't even sure in the beginning if I could handle working. Before I returned to work, we put things in place in case I wasn't able to manage the job.

Denise and I both had life insurance. One of my really good friends, a guy I used to work with, covered my life and auto insurance. I'm pretty sure I was the first insurance policy he ever wrote. When I met Denise and we moved in together, we added her life insurance as well as our homeowners' policy through him. After Denise died, I vividly remember sitting between Dirk and my dad and being handed a check for more money than I've ever received, all while crying and waiting to be seated at the Cheesecake Factory.

At the time, I just felt like it was blood money. If I had taken the doctor's office to court, any settlement I would have received would have been blood money too. It represented the blood that was spilled, the loss of everything I held dear. I didn't want the money but knew I needed to accept it in case I was ever not able to earn my living.

I gave some to the church, some to the memorial fund, and stuck some in savings for the car as well. My financial advisor, my dad, and I sat down one evening to talk about the money. We decided we would put five years' worth of mortgage payments in the bank on the off chance that I wasn't able to hold down a job. It was truly a smart decision. That would see me through enough time to get back on my feet. Fortunately, I was able to return to work and did so well with my kids thanks to a great deal of help from my administration and colleagues. I gave the rest of the money to my financial advisor, Ricky, and our goal is for me to never use it until retirement.

After I returned to work and settled into my routines following Denise's death, taking care of the house came next. Thankfully, Denise's mother and sister kindly dealt with Denise's closet and the nursery. We were doing our best to manage things after the tragedy as best we could. Beyond clearing out her closet and the nursery, I didn't make any changes to the house during those first couple of years. I kept the decor exactly the way Denise had wanted it. Although Denise's parents cleaned and made some small alterations, everything remained as it had been the day before our world was shattered.

Few changes took place in the years that followed. In the upstairs space between bedrooms, I created a wall display with five of my favorite photos of Denise and me. I also added some more photos of Denise to the master bedroom. Apart from those minor variations, the house remained a reflection of Denise.

The house was in an ideal location. I was able to put my shoes on and go run or walk whenever I wanted. At one point, I ended up running a marathon around the neighborhood, completing three loops. Having a neighbor like Adam made the area where we lived much better. Adam always checked up on me. I'll always remember that evening at the viewing when he looked my parents in the eye and told them he would be there for me. Well, he definitely didn't lie.

As beautiful and well situated as the home was, at no point after Denise passed did anyone think my future was in that house. We all understood that I would be living there in the present and in the near future, but one way or another at a certain point, I was going to sell the house.

I wasn't ready for a long time. After about two and a half years, I started to recognize how hard it would be for people to visit and look at all Denise's knickknacks. I kept the pictures on the walls but moved the little keepsakes and small photos from the TV stands both upstairs and downstairs into another room.

When the house was built, we had the option of a screened-in porch but decided it was too expensive. Denise's parents turned their back porch into a beautiful sunroom. I mentioned that to mom one time on a visit, and she said she would pay for it if I found someone to do the same with our back porch. Denise's dad laid down some outdoor carpet. All-purpose windows were installed, and there were electrical outlets; it was pretty impressive. I got a pair of wicker chairs and a sofa for the space, ordered sports blankets, and bought an oscillating fan and heater so I could be out there as much as I wanted.

Mom and I both agreed it was a great decision because now there was at least one place in the house that was mine. I bought the furniture and decorated the sunroom, which was more or less my contribution to the house. My mom was so kind to pay for it.

Over time, I continued to make minor improvements to the house. I bought a couple of canvases of places I had been with my parents and put those in the downstairs living room. Since I spent much of my time away from school in that house, I tried to make it livable. Around the three-year mark, which was the second year of our relay race, I suggested that our running team have a Christmas party, and most of them seemed interested. I said I would host since I had a decent-sized house and was more than happy for people to come in. The relay team agreed, so I sent out an electronic invitation and a Christmas party date was set.

About a month before the party, my mom was in town. She finally had agreed to let me take her to Cameron Indoor Stadium to see a Duke University basketball game. She had a really good time.

During her stay, I asked her what she thought about the photos I had hanging of Denise. Mom thought if I was going to have people over to the house, it would probably be best if I took them down. Hosting the party essentially forced me to do something that I had been needing to do for a while, to change the inside of the house.

We took down the photos of Denise in the upstairs hallway and added some new pictures to those frames. I also bought additional canvases for the upstairs loft and the master bedroom. After three years, I was finally ready to make this change. It was tough but needed to be done.

The party went really well. Everyone seemed to have fun. My Jeopardy knock-off trivia game was mediocre, but the honey-baked ham I bought seemed to make up for the failed game.

The only real symbol of Denise that was visible in the main areas of the house was the framed wedding attendee picture that we had people sign. Other than that, the house now held some of my own style. As difficult as it had been to alter what was, the time was finally right for me to let go of the way things had been.

When the pandemic hit, I proved to myself that I could stay in that house for extended periods of time and remain functional. Only by recognizing the strides I had made did I become capable of making those next steps forward.

I was lying in bed reading one night when I got a text from my friend Melissa. She and Thomas Royer continued to be supportive, caring, helpful, and enjoyable people to be around. She texted me that they were looking at my in-laws' house since it was on the market, but they didn't like it. Denise's parents' home was lovely as well, and they had a really great upstairs loft. However, because the loft was so large, the bedrooms were smaller. Melissa and Thomas already had two kids and a third on the way, so they needed bigger bedrooms. I mentioned that they were more than welcome to look at my house. I knew that both Melissa and Thomas had been inside the house but maybe not upstairs. I knew by then that my future wasn't in that house.

Neither of us texted or reached out for about a month. But one weekend, they invited me to their street for some brisket. Thomas was close to the guys next door, and they bought a brisket that was going to be cooking all day. I told them I'd be more than happy to come over and help them eat such tasty food.

At one point, it started to rain, so we grabbed what we could and went into their house. I had been in the Royer's home a number of times because they were all, including the kids, really compassionate and had me over to hang out, eat dinner, and go to sporting events on many occasions after Denise's death. Once we were indoors in the kitchen, Thomas said, "Melissa said that you were interested in selling your house." He observed me intently to gauge my reaction to the question.

I told Thomas I had finally reached a place of understanding that I would be able to move. I told him I didn't mention the possibility again after my text because I didn't want them to feel uncomfortable about looking at my house.

He said they would be interested in looking at my house since they had never really spent time checking each of the rooms with an intention of possibly moving there. I told him I knew my future wasn't in that house and that I would love for it to go to someone who would love the home and treat it the way Denise and I would have.

A few days later, the Royers and their real estate agent walked through the house. Shortly afterward, they said they would be interested in purchasing the house.

Even though I sold my first house through Denise's friend, who was also our realtor, I didn't know the first thing about selling homes or discussing an asking price. I didn't have a realtor as my house really wasn't on the market. When I told this to the Royers, they just calmly invited me to come over that week for dinner to talk.

The spaghetti was delicious, and the kids were always really happy to see me. After Melissa and the kids went upstairs, Thomas and I got down to business. He is an intelligent lawyer and I'm neither of those things, so I was curious to see how the conversation would unfold. As brilliant as Thomas is, he is equally easy to talk to. Many extremely smart people don't have the ability to converse with anyone on any level but Thomas does.

His realtor had given Thomas the price she would suggest for my house if she were my agent. Of course, I wouldn't come away with the full asking price because of realtor fees. Thomas proposed a flat price that was more than I would have made *with* a realtor but would also cost less for them. It was a perfect plan. I would make more money and they would pay less because I didn't have a realtor. I agreed and felt that would be a perfect solution. He said his realtor could get all the paperwork and closing documents together and the lawyer, and I simply needed to get the house clean and give them the keys.

What an ideal plan. I could get a fair price for the house with no realtor fees or months of showings while also showing how much this meant to me. Within about a week, I had signed the contract, and all that was left to figure out was where to move.

As soon as the possibility of selling arose, I started thinking about what I might need to do. I had time on weekends to start packing everything up, which is exactly what I did. I bought some clear containers and began to determine and sort the things I wanted to keep.

I had several conversations with my dad about where to live. Between the money I had in savings from the mortgage and life insurance, the funds I had added to that, plus the money from selling the house, I *could* end up buying a new home. But I didn't think that was the smart choice. I felt the right thing to do was to go full reset.

I wanted and needed to reset much of my life. I reached out to a close friend who lived in an apartment complex and asked if she minded if I moved into the complex. She was fine with that idea, so within about a month after my conversation with the Royers, I had a one bedroom/one bathroom apartment in a different town. Downsizing forced me to keep only what I needed in hopes that down the road I could build a different life.

Selling the house finally gave me the chance to go back through everything that was given to me the week of Denise's passing. I had kept all of it in the chest of drawers in our bedroom. I read over all the notes from the viewing, every card that was sent to me, and every paper that came my way. It was beneficial to look back and recall all those who had cared for me so early in my grief. I made packets for Denise's family and friends and put them to the side to pass them along when the time came. It was a therapeutic way to say goodbye to the house.

As horrible as COVID-19 was, it gave me the chance to take my time and look through everything. I remember that first year, sitting in the loft and looking at every photo I had of Denise and just crying. Now I was sorting through everything to figure out what I would keep and what I would pass along. I knew I had to let go of a lot, but I wanted to save the most important items.

All my belongings were put into clear containers for easy access at my next place. I knew I wouldn't need to unpack everything after the move since I planned on only being at the apartment for about six months.

The house had four bedrooms, a living room, breakfast nook, dining room, sunroom, and an upstairs loft. Clearly, not all of the furniture was going to fit into my one-bedroom apartment. In some strange way, I felt good about letting go of much of it. I would enjoy buying new furniture down the road to build a new life. That furniture represented my life and my dreams for the future with Denise, which sadly never happened. I asked the Royers what they wanted, and they took a couple of sofas, a chest of drawers, a dining table, and our upstairs sectional in the loft.

I reached out to all my friends who had been so good to me to see what they wanted to take. I told everyone I didn't want any money, that this was my way of saying thank you for their support and kindness. My friend Lindsay chose a couple of new chests of drawers, and my amazing coworker Jeannie took a couple of living room chairs and an ottoman. I let go of spare beds, a dining room table, an office desk, and a bookshelf. I gave it all away. The only furniture I kept for the apartment was my elliptical, my wicker chairs and sofa, my bed, a couple of bookshelves, a filing cabinet, the washer and dryer, and a few folding tables. That was all. However, I kept the TVs as I didn't want to go full minimalist.

It felt good giving everything away. Whatever I wasn't going to keep I either donated or let people come and take.

Originally, my dad and I had planned to travel to Munich, Germany, during that time. With everything shutting down, that wasn't going to happen, so my dad came to visit instead. Needless to say, it was great having him there. During his stay, we had people in to paint and fix a few small things, and I didn't need to take time off of work to let them in since he was there. Dad also finished one of my last projects, which was the kitchen. We laid out all the kitchen utensils and items that Denise had used (clearly I wasn't the baker; she was), and people came over and grabbed whatever they wanted. Giving these things to friends was a way to thank them. Denise's father even came over to fill in all the holes in the walls left from the pictures. We all pitched in and got the house in order to turn over to the new homeowners.

The Royers felt inclined to pay me for the furniture pieces they received, but I really didn't want anything. They were insistent about paying me, so we finally agreed upon whatever they thought was a fair price being cut down the middle with half going to me and the other half being added to their kids' college scholarship fund.

The most difficult item to deal with was Denise's chest, which had been crafted lovingly by her father. I didn't have room for it in the apartment. He was justly disappointed that I wasn't taking it with me. Keeping it would have meant a lot to me, but that wasn't practical under the circumstances. We put the chest and everything else for Denise's family into their cars.

There were keepsakes from Denise that I took with me as well. I bought two gray containers to hold the most memorable, meaningful items that I will probably keep for the rest of my life. One container held five years' worth of cards from all the holidays since Denise passed, our wedding album, and the blanket Denise's mother had quilted out of all the T-shirts Denise had collected from the places we had been during our time together. The second container housed all of my writings to Denise after she died, all of our photo books, the items from the viewing and funeral, the Run for Dee Dee 5K T-shirts I got for her as well as some other important and meaningful pieces. I also unframed the signed wedding attendee photo and rolled that up to keep along with my favorite wreath Denise made.

Once the house was cleaned and I settled into my new apartment, I gave the house keys to the Royers early and they started moving things over. They still have me over to the house. Seeing how much they are enjoying it with their three little kids is a really full circle moment for me. They are a great family. It means the world to me that I was able to pass that beautiful house on to such great people.

Sadly, I'm not hosting too many parties these days as my wicker sofa and folding chairs aren't exactly ideal for social gatherings. However, the full reset was the perfect way to handle the transition from my life with Denise to whatever my future holds. The fact that the house we shared is being treated with the love and respect Denise and I would have given it brings me comfort. Most importantly, I think Denise would be proud of me for the way things with the house turned out. Knowing it belongs to people as great as the Royers means a great deal.

Chapter 18
Being in Public

When I found Denise, the love of my life, I thought my dating days were over. I enjoyed being married and was thankful I no longer had to play the game of "Do you like me or not?"

When Denise died, I was completely alone and depressed. I'd love to forget that time in my life, but I also hope I will never forget. I believe we come to understand more about ourselves during the painful periods than we do in the good times. I certainly learned who my real friends were after tragedy struck my life. The experience of being so alone when people didn't know how to talk to me will stay with me for a long while. Thankfully, as time passes, I can look back on those desperate times and recognize how far I've come.

Losing Denise was gut-wrenching. Facing a life without her was inconceivable. I was in no shape to move forward with my life. I only knew that I was desperately alone. I thought my life was over.

As months turned into years of loneliness, however, I finally realized that dating would have to become a part of my life again at some point. The prospect was made even more dreadful by all the baggage I now carried. I had never been great at meeting new people, but I would have to face that prospect if I wanted a second chance at life.

I was painfully aware of how truly unhealthy I was to be around. The lack of any consistent, day-to-day support was a clear sign that people's lives were better without me. I am not blaming anyone for this. The fact is that most people my age had lives, families, and kids while I lost all of that in a single night.

I wasn't in the right mindset to date for a long time, but eventually I had to make a choice to escape a life of utter loneliness. I never thought a friend was likely to introduce me to someone because of the tragedy that still colored my world. Beyond that, I think if you polled an average number of people with the question of how long it would take someone to get over the kind of loss I had suffered, most people would say multiple years or that it might never happen. I couldn't imagine a future where my friends would feel comfortable trying to set me up with a woman they knew. I mean, who wants to tell a friend, "I have this wonderful guy, but there is one catch: he lost his whole world."

Eventually, I made the choice to create a passive dating profile. I have always struggled with the idea of promoting myself. Trying to describe my positive characteristics felt awkward. Who wants to read the dating profile of the man who lost his entire life? "Single male seeks interest to help him get over the passing of his wife and unborn kids." That isn't exactly a *normal* dating profile. Had that actually been my profile, at least it would have been honest, a quality that isn't seen a lot on dating sites.

Regardless, I created a profile and started to seek companionship. I hated being judged by others and found the idea of doing the same to others distasteful. The entire experience made me feel uncomfortable.

I continued to overanalyze my thoughts, feelings, and actions. I'm extremely self-reflective and during that time I reflected on how weak I was. After about six months, I finally had enough and quit the website. I rejoined three months later after the loneliness again started to eat away at me.

I went back and forth multiple times and really only met one person with whom I felt a connection, Kami. She reached out to me because we were both widows. I hadn't met any widows my age and was filled with mixed feelings when she contacted me, so I waited before replying. We have quite different spiritual beliefs, so we agreed we would meet as friends, which was exactly the right thing to do.

I drove to meet Kami one weekend afternoon for coffee (I had tea because I don't drink coffee) and we talked. Ninety-nine percent of the world would probably have considered our conversation extremely depressing, but for us it was uplifting. Kami's story is similar to mine in that we have both faced genuine sadness. Although I was taught not to compare my grief to anyone else's, in this case it was clear that Kami and I were very much on the same wavelength. What probably made Kami's story more difficult was the fact that she had two kids to support. As tough as my situation was, I couldn't even imagine trying to keep myself together while being there for two children who were also grieving.

Since I got to the cafe first, I sat facing outward into the crowd while Kami faced me and the wall behind me. We talked openly about each of our stories, discussed things that made our lives better and worse, and conversed about where we currently felt we were on our grief journey. Because she had her back turned to the people nearby, what Kami never saw was how our conversation affected others. I noticed on multiple occasions those faces reveal expressions of sadness.

Kami and I spoke honestly and openly about situations that other people couldn't imagine. What I tend to forget in those moments is that people around us may overhear our conversation. These unlucky individuals were just trying to enjoy a nice time out with their families and had the misfortune to sit near us.

While I wish I could have saved these strangers from those moments of distress, I understand the value of not shying away from a public environment during times of grief. I didn't make a point to tell Kami about what I saw over her shoulder. I was sad that these people were affected by what we were dealing with but grateful that I wasn't trying to further isolate myself in a world that still didn't make sense.

Toward the end of our conversation, Kami mentioned that she and other widows often had dinner together and said she felt I would be a welcome addition to their group. I was overjoyed that she appreciated our conversation enough to invite me to spend time around people my age who had stories similar to mine. Until I met Kami, I didn't really have a widow support system among likeminded people my age. This was an important step I was glad to take.

Since meeting Kami, I have become involved with our widow's group. We have an exclusive text thread and continue to get together once every couple of months. The group includes me and three wonderful women who have lost their husbands. We are tightknit, honest, and open. We ask each other questions and push each other to continue to grow. They are all wonderful, supportive people. (Carol and Carolyn, your friendship means the world to me.)

There are certain moments that, as was the case with the house, seem to come full circle. One of those came within the last six months. Carol, Carolyn, and I were able to witness Kami get married on the beach. It was a wonderful moment, and we all were so thrilled to see her look as beautiful and happy as she was that day. I had never met Kami's husband. He had attended one of our dinners, but I wasn't able to be there at that state of the pandemic. I tried to limit my exposure as I continued to teach. However, because this was a smaller wedding with only family and true friends, the three of us widows (Carol, Carolyn, and me) made the cut. I was happy to meet Kami's husband, who was incredibly lucky to marry such a wonderful, kind, brilliant, and beautiful woman.

Around the widows, I can be myself. I don't have to pretend to be happy. I can be honest. If I were to sit down and have dinner with them and pretend that everything was great, they would call me out on it. The four of us are in this together and care deeply for each other. We share tears, smiles, laughs, moments of joy, and times of sorrow. Most importantly, we are a support system for each other and value each other's honest and caring friendship.

When I took myself off the dating websites, I did so because I wasn't in the right frame of mind to find someone. If I had tried to force myself into a relationship in order to escape loneliness, I would felt as much guilt as I would have experienced had I sold the house too soon. Also, it was important for me to become independent, to function on my own, before trying to get into a relationship. I do want a relationship and have shared my feelings of interest with someone, but for right now I'm extremely comfortable with where I am.

I am not proud of how weak I was. I tried to mask my pain by seeking companionship on a dating website. Although I really only met Kami in the process during those trying times, what I paid to be on the site was worth every penny to gain that friendship. I found a loyal friend who guided me to our widow's group. No one wants to join a widow's group, but each of us is thankful to support one another.

Another aspect of public life relates to my continued attempts to make the world a better place and to not let Denise's story die. I felt the world could learn a great deal from what happened to my wife. There is true value in listening to patients, showing them their doctors care for them, and there's a better way for the medical community to handle death. Although I think my message is powerful, people, companies, and businesses aren't lining up on my doorstep to give me a microphone.

Since this tragedy took place, I believed our story could affect change. Education is one way out of the darkness. However, this reality is so dark and filled with sorrow that people often don't want to acknowledge such events. Because the data said Denise was fine, no lawyer would take the case (given that laws are not written in favor of people like me), but I believe this story could happen to anyone. Our story was so terrible that calls or emails requesting to be heard often fell on deaf ears. A truth I hold close to my heart is that, if we don't learn from our mistakes, then are we really trying to be better? I think we could all agree that mistakes were made—some on my end and some by others. If we don't have honest and open conversations, then Denise and those babies died for nothing. Their story goes away and no one cares.

Clearly I care deeply, but my story becomes less impactful with the passing of time. If I stood in front of a medical conference after one year, my story would be rawer, more powerful, and more charged with emotion than it could be after five years. My first book revealed that kind of rawness because I wrote it during the most intense period of grief. I wanted to get my voice, drenched in pain, out into the world at the one-year mark for that reason.

Because I understood this, I tried early on to speak to groups. I was fortunate to talk to the social work program at a college here in town. The talk centered around the professor's lesson about taking care of yourself in order to help others. In social work, you have to deal with a lot of other people's situations, but that's impossible unless you find ways to cope with your own problems.

I spoke to two classes about what I was going through and answered all their questions. I think they were shocked by how open and honest I was. The questions they asked were the same ones I asked myself at home. The only difference was I had people to listen. I felt I could have done the presentation better, but I believe I left each student with something to think about and felt proud of what I had said.

Through my friend Kami, I also was given a chance to speak to a class of nurses. Kami had a friend who taught nurses and reached out to her after I told her that I felt my story could help others. I think I presented my story well but still could have done better. It's the weirdest thing looking around a room and talking from your heart and smiling because you see people cry. It wasn't my intention to make anyone cry, but their tears meant I had reached them, that the death of Denise and our unborn twins and the path of grief I experienced afterward affected them. Seeing people care, even through their tears, made me realize I could in some small way make the world better.

These experiences, which were arranged by friends or friends of a friend, were wonderful, and I was glad I had an opportunity to speak to both of these classes and schools. But I felt it was important for me to branch out and talk to medical conferences.

When I first met my friend Jared during my teacher training, I was drafting an email to a medical conference. I had sent multiple emails to conferences without reply. Even hearing "no thanks" would have been welcome. I never got a response. Not once did I ever hear, "We as so sorry for what you are going through, but unfortunately we don't have the appropriate forum for you." All of my emails ended up in their trash.

Every time I don't hear back, that inner demon of mental illness says, "See, they don't care about you." As much as I try to fight that voice, it gets louder the more I attempt to reach out in this effort to make the world a better place.

At one point, I got tired of putting my trust in the medical community and got the idea that maybe adults couldn't change their minds, that maybe the best place to start shifting attitudes was when people were younger and more impressionable. I sent emails to two impressive universities, both with medical schools.

I got a response from the University of North Carolina (UNC) within a couple of days. The medical lead replied that he was truly sorry about my story, that he would forward the email to one of his colleagues and that I should hear back shortly. That silenced the inner demon for a bit.

I heard from this colleague, and within the week we set up an appointment for me to drive there and meet with her in person. I got permission to leave work early and went to meet her. She was pleasant, incredibly smart, knowledgeable, and, most importantly, caring. She asked questions, and I told her the whole story. She seemed to understand where I was coming from and felt that UNC students would benefit from hearing about what happened. I felt relieved that finally someone *saw* me, met with and vetted me, and believed I could help others. Even if someone had investigated me and then said, "No thanks," I couldn't be mad. At least they gave me a chance. Until that appointment, no one had ever given me that opportunity. I cried in front of her, and she could see how much I cared. She said that I would hear from her and that she wanted to see what she could do and what would be best.

True to her word, she contacted me, and I was given the chance to speak to an early medical school class. I was overwhelmed that someone believed in my story and in me enough to give me an outlet to speak about what had happened and to do my part to keep this tragedy from occurring again.

I took off the day of the talk from school and arrived early. I went into the building to use the facilities before returning outside to walk for a while to settle my anxieties. When it was almost time to begin, I grabbed my water and walked into the classroom. I sat while a doctor talked about mortality rates for mothers and the students asked questions. Then it was my turn.

I took a moment to breathe as I looked around at all the young faces and then just started talking. I began telling them how Denise and I met and then shared about our attempts to get pregnant. I talked about how happy we were when we found out we were going to have twins, a boy and a girl. The students realized my story didn't end with the joyful outcome of their birth. When I went into detail about their tragic ending, I believe my words affected them. We talked about how things were handled or mishandled with regard to support and how convoluted things can become when legalities come into play. The students seemed to respond. As exhausted as I was after telling the story, I felt gratified when a couple of the students thanked me at the end of class. The professors said I did a good job, and I sincerely thanked them for giving me a chance to share the story.

They took a chance on me and gave me an outlet. Even if the opportunity never came again, what those professors did for me was everything. I am forever grateful to UNC for giving me a chance to affect some change and do my small part to make sure there is not another Denise.

I felt overwhelmed when I got a follow-up email to thank me and tell me the students seemed to learn from my talk. It meant even more when they told me they wanted me to return. I have gone back every year since to the same class. I will forever be grateful for their belief in me and that they share my view that education is the way forward.

I am always mindful that these are students just beginning a potential career in medicine. One year, when the associate professor walked me to the classroom, I mentioned recognizing that these were early medical students and said I wanted to avoid bringing everything down on them by discussing my views about the legal side of medicine. He knew what I meant and appreciated how I saw the big picture. He was always supportive and seemed to really care.

They also invited me to speak to their big OB/GYN class and even encouraged me to discuss the legal issues concerning Denise's death. Sadly, the pandemic took away my chance to tell my story to their almost graduated OB/GYN students. It would have been a great opportunity, but I was still grateful to the university for believing in me. I wish more places felt the same way. Regardless, UNC will always be a world-class institution, and I'm fortunate they gave me a chance. From the bottom of my heart, thank you, UNC.

One would think that might have opened more doors, but it hasn't. Now, when I email other institutions, I mention that I have spoken at UNC and also tell them they can read my first book to discover the kind of person I am. Still, UNC seems to be the only university so far that agrees with my stance on learning from such tragedies.

I'm not as devastated when I don't hear back now. Maybe that's because I have lowered my expectations. Maybe I'm just more guarded. The fact that at least one place believed in me and even asked me to return gave me a sense of meaning and restored my belief that my story can make a difference. I hope there never will be another story like Denise's and that my efforts will continue to have an effect.

Speaking in public and being the center of attention remains uncomfortable for me, but I believe in the power of the story and that it would be selfish not to share it if it can change even one life for the better. When I talk about Denise, about her death and the death of our babies, I find a way to get through my discomfort because I truly believe in the story and its tragic lesson.

Chapter 19

Reflections of a Father

My name is Randy Moore, and I am the father of Levi. Since Denise passed, my wife Brenda and I have watched our son struggle through the most tragic time of his life. Levi was not prepared to be widowed at such an early age. Bill, Judy, Dawn, Brian, and Sara were not prepared to lose a loved one so young. And Brenda and I were not prepared to deal with the death of a daughter-in-law and the aftermath that our son had to endure.

Brenda and I live in Tennessee. A few days after Denise's funeral, Brenda drove back there, and I stayed a few weeks with Levi. Very slowly, Levi and I started tackling some of the immediate endeavors that had to be dealt with. Sometimes Levi was not ready to discuss things. Other times, he and I worked well together. If we accomplished one thing a day, we felt productive.

One of the first endeavors was to secure estate lawyers to help us understand how to proceed with the financial part of Levi's new life. Luckily, a widowed friend of Levi's steered us to local estate attorneys she had used. They were extra accommodating to Levi since most of their customers were heirs who were much older and knowledgeable about the handling of estates.

Levi and I also had a series of discussions on returning to work. A friend of his had written that a friend of hers was also a young widower. That person had gone back to work but stayed only a brief time that first day. She never went back and eventually resigned from her position. (We may only hope she found employment that she could manage later in her life.) Levi had always liked his teaching career, and I knew someday he would need to go back. His school principal was quite accommodating regarding his return, so there was little pressure. But I felt the longer Levi waited, the harder it would be.

Levi and I decided on the day. He left for school, knowing he could call me at any time to pick him up if needed. I knew the entire day for Levi was difficult, but my day was also trying. I kept thinking that I had pushed Levi into going back to work too soon. I also worried the entire day that the phone would ring, and I would need to pick Levi up from school. I was quite relieved when Levi walked into the house after his full day at school.

I tried not to ask too many questions, but Levi was willing to discuss some of his day. He did better than he thought he would. The principal and staff were gracious, but the kids were the charm. They said how sorry they were and then went on with their youthful lives. Levi continued to head to school each morning from then on. Occasionally, he would say that going back to school was the best thing he could have done. That meant a great deal to me.

I eventually needed to head back to my home. I knew Brenda had planned to come over in a few weeks. Levi took me to the airport, and I quickly unloaded my baggage and headed into the terminal. Neither one of us needed a lengthy goodbye. I remember on the flight that I had the same feeling as when Levi went back to school that first day. Maybe I was leaving Levi too soon.

I returned three months later for another extended visit. An additional endeavor for that visit was the selling of Denise's car. Levi did not need two vehicles. His SUV was plenty. But selling a car under this circumstance was extremely hard. He had asked a family member about Denise's car, but that person did not need it. Levi decided against selling the car himself. One morning, I followed him to a place where cars are bought and sold. They gave him a reasonable offer and he took it. In no time, an important part of Denise's life was removed from Levi's.

Between then and now, Brenda and I have visited Levi on many occasions, and he has also come to see us. And the telephone is a lifesaver. The Caller-ID setup on my phone, though, never felt the same. When I saw Levi calling, my stomach went into a knot. Sometimes he was happy and sounded like his old self. But at other times, he was angry or sad and spent most of the call crying. Every time I saw his name on the Caller-ID, I worried about who I was going to talk to. Eventually, his telephone calls were much calmer. By now, he is back to his old self on the phone.

Last year, Levi sold his house to friends. This was the place he and Denise had built and was supposed to be their dream home for their family for a long time. Unfortunately, upon Denise's death, this house became the place of nightmares. Denise had decorated their home from top to bottom, and it was beautiful. But at the same time, it held all the pain of this devastating loss.

Levi knew soon after Denise's death that the house would be sold eventually. Luckily, Levi had enough finances to stay until he was ready to move. After four years, it was time to sell. I helped Levi in the process of donating many items as he prepared to move to an apartment. Another part of Denise's life was removed from Levi's existence.

At the time of this writing, Levi has been in his apartment for 18 months. In the future I hope he can purchase another house. I would like to see him continue to move forward. When that happens, I know his precious memories of Denise and her "great smile" will remain. Although many of the objects that represented her life are gone, Levi will hold in his heart all the moments and the treasures of their love.

Chapter 20

Denise's Legacy

Denise was a truly inspiring teacher and person who always made those around her *better*. She deserved to be given the world, but the world didn't hold up its end of the bargain. Countless people were devastated by her death. Seeing the outpouring of love that Denise's family and I experienced at the funeral was in its own way a celebration of how great she was.

More times than I can count, I've wished I could travel back in time to change the outcome of her life. After she died, I also wished I could fast-forward my own life to a time when I wasn't in so much pain. I envisioned a time similar to where I am now on the journey through grief. I will always feel sorrow for what should have been, but I'm not as desperate, alone, and depressed as I was.

I worked really hard to get to where I am now. I have taken the long road and believe now that was the right path for me. Looking back on the last five years, I feel how massive a step I made in coming to a point where I am comfortable with myself. I know that things should have turned out differently, but I can't change the past. I can only change where I am in the present and hope to make the future better.

Denise was and forever will be part of who I am. She shaped my life, my world, and my being beyond measure. I hope I will always carry some of her greatness inside of me. I also hope that all those who knew her or were taught by Denise will remember the person she was. We are the ones who carry her legacy forward. May we pay tribute to her memory by living courageously, honorably, creatively, and kindly.

When Denise died, we were fortunate to receive help in setting up the Denise H. Moore Memorial Fund to help carry on Denise's legacy by supporting worthy causes. Those who showed their love through thoughtful and generous donations sustain her legacy in such a meaningful way. Denise's family and I remain forever grateful.

The fund is still going strong, and we continue to use donations to support charities and positive causes we know Denise believed in as well as others we believe she would have loved. We gave money to her school and continue to encourage teachers there to get their National Board Certification. Before she passed, we celebrated with family when Denise received this additional add-on certificate, which meant a lot to her. I'm grateful we had that occasion to celebrate her before the universe took her away.

Our fund continues to donate to multiple school libraries every year. Denise was an avid reader. She was the one who recommended many of the books I have read. I recall one of our staff meetings at the beginning of the school year when the theme was a book Denise already had showed me. I barely managed to make it outside before I started crying when that happened. The fact that she already knew this book was further proof that Denise was so far ahead of all of us with her caring and compassionate thinking.

Denise was a coach for an organization called Girls on the Run, an after-school program that encourages girls to gain strengths and confidence by preparing to complete a 5K run. Denise loved the organization, and we continue to award scholarships to girls who wouldn't have the financial means to join the group otherwise.

I am not the person who writes the checks. I enjoy being the person who provides ideas and talks to companies about how we can support them. There was tension earlier on, when our feelings were so raw, about some of my email and fund requests not getting submitted, but those concerns have been eliminated.

I've run a couple of races in town to benefit an organization, Healing Transitions, that helps people who have fallen on hard times get back on their feet. With her compassionate soul, Denise would have wanted to support them, so we donate to their good cause as well.

Much of the money in our fund is contributed to people and organizations that are trying to make the world a better place. We like to find groups that are helping those less fortunate because we know that's where Denise's heart was. If she had this money, she would donate to these kinds of organizations. Denise always had a generous, loving heart. We seek to keep her compassionate nature alive by using her fund to make a positive impact.

The Run for Dee Dee 5k also brought in donations to Denise's fund. Almost nine months after Denise and the babies passed away, we were able to organize a race that benefited the memorial fund and raised awareness for the beautiful soul Denise was.

Our 5K has had some ups and downs, but overall we were fortunate to hold the race for four successful years. When the pandemic hit, we essentially lost two years' worth of fundraising with the race. In truth, though, our race was more about the community and less about trying to raise money. I cared more about people having a good time and getting kids involved than raising money. That might have been one of the shortfalls of the race, but we weren't a huge race in any case, and part of me wanted it to be about the people.

By the third year, I had an extremely difficult time hearing back from my two friends who were so good early on about helping with the timing of the race. For whatever reason, they just stopped communicating with me. I'm sure they were too scared to let me know that, while they wanted to help early on to support me, the time commitment away from their families was too much to continue. I wish they would have just been honest with me.

That same third year, I got called into a meeting in the town's city building. Apparently, the town was planning a community event that included a race with the local running club. They realized that I already had reserved their desired race date for our race. I didn't mind letting them have that date as long as I could get another race date. Afterward, the two gentlemen from the running club and I had a beer together. They had researched what our race was about and wanted to help. They were able to provide the timing for our race since I had not heard from those who normally helped plan our 5k.

We ended up finding a different race date that actually was a little challenging because the park where we run was pretty busy during that time frame. Our race was due to begin much earlier in the day than we would have liked. It would be dark right up until race time, so I bought enough little lantern flashlights for people to see while getting their race packets and warming up.

The race always seemed to be an enjoyable time for everyone. It was also an opportunity to reflect on the passing of Denise and the twins in a way that wasn't so sad.

At one point, I was called by some of Denise's parents' friends. They reached out with an idea that I never really had considered. This retired couple, the Joyces, said they would like to get sponsorships for the race and help in any way they could. They mentioned it was incredibly difficult for Denise's parents to go to various companies and restaurants and pour their hearts out over and over in order to gain sponsorships. I had never considered how hard that would be for them but certainly understood.

I would have tried to bring in sponsors, but my work schedule made the time commitment too difficult. Since Denise's parents were retired, they had more time to go to these places, talk to the managers, and tell the story that led us to hold the race. The Joyces explained that pouring out their hearts to these strangers only to have them not be able to provide sponsorship was devastating to Denise's parents.

The Joyces were thoughtful and observant in seeing how tough it was on Denise's parents. I gave the couple the go-ahead to do whatever they wanted in terms of gaining sponsors. They did an amazing job and generated more revenue than we ever made. They also helped with something else that I had wanted to do if I ever got the chance.

Most races reward the fastest runner. However, being different from most, I always wanted to reward the slowest. Those fast runners were admirable, of course, but the true value in our 5K races came from inviting people to participate who wouldn't get up and exercise without this cause. The people who ran regularly weren't challenged to finish a quick 3.1 miles. However, for participants who didn't normally run, just completing the race was impressive. We offered awards for a couple of years because I wanted to prove we could put on a "normal" race. However, the following year and going forward, we were able to do a raffle for door prizes that went to almost everyone who attended.

When the Joyces spoke to companies that weren't able to sponsor, they asked if they could donate gift cards or coupons for the raffle. That became a great success. We even got the local educational science museum to donate a four-person gift certificate. It was a wonderful way to end the race. Another benefit of the raffle was that I didn't have to do anything.

One of my major intentions was that I always wanted the race to be a reflection of Denise, not of me. I would walk away from the race if I felt it was becoming about me. I liked doing all the background work, getting the facilities, ordering the bibs, T-shirts, medals, and helping to organize it. I didn't mind saying something before the race, but once the runners started running, I loved just watching. That was my favorite part. When we were lucky with the weather and had no injuries, the 5k was a wonderful experience that I enjoyed and loved.

I was delighted by how involved we got the kids. We offered those who didn't plan to run but wanted to donate the opportunity to "sponsor a kid." We tried to organize it to include kids who ran for free. I would try to use those free spots for as many kids from different schools as I could, but it became challenging.

Another positive component for me was getting to pick the race colors for the first two years. That first year we chose red for Denise's master's degree from North Carolina State, and the second year we opted for blue to commemorate her undergraduate degree from Florida Atlantic University. After that, I felt the kids should decide. I approached the wonderful leader of the student council at school, my truly esteemed colleague and friend Jeannie, who took it to the student council and let them decide the race colors. The third year of the event they picked green and the next year, which was the failed coronavirus year, they chose purple. I loved the idea that we were trying to incorporate as many children into the planning process as we could. We loved all the adults who came, but the race was for the kids. We had kids who ran and others who volunteered, and my wonderful dear friend made sure everyone got a medal at the end. I'm really proud of what we did with that race.

Unfortunately, as time went on and people's lives got busy, not everyone could make the yearly commitment. I felt it becoming more of a reflection of me than Denise at that point, so as a family we decided against continuing the race. During the coronavirus, we had no idea when we would have had the race if we had continued. Although it was sad letting this part of her legacy go, looking back, it was nonetheless impressive how well the family came together and worked as a group in making that race what it was.

I always knew that I wanted to keep some form of tradition alive even if we didn't have a formal race. I had to order all the medals well in advance and always purchased extra medals beyond what we needed to keep for other occasions. I have used a few with my friend Eileen when we put on our fun running events with friends. But I still wanted to have one day where we celebrated Denise.

The year I gave up the race date to the town and their local running club, I settled on having our race the first Saturday of April. That was going to be our race date in the future. After we discontinued our official race, I let everyone know that if they wanted to come to the adjacent park to where we used to have the race and run, walk, skip, or push a baby stroller, I would have a medal for them. I covered the flat side of our old medals with that year's sticker for anyone who wanted one and didn't ask for any money. It was simply a way to give back to all those who had supported us and to have at least one day to honor Denise's memory. It began the Unofficial Run for Dee Dee 5k. Frankly, Denise deserves far more than a single day, but we all live busy lives, and acknowledging her even then keeps her memory alive.

Denise's legacy may continue through our informal race on the first Saturday of April as well as our memorial fund, but, most importantly, those who knew her carry a little bit of her inside our hearts. Denise improved the lives of everyone around her. The world was a brighter place when she was in it.

Denise was a tireless teacher and a true advocate for all of her students. I still remember all those evenings sitting beside her on the couch while she continued to do school work with her computer on her lap as I selfishly played on my phone or watched a movie. She cared deeply about everyone, and the fact that she is gone is a tragedy. Denise was an outstanding role model for her students and brought out the best in everyone including me.

I recently met another widow, Amber, who is doing much better than I am. She and I have had many open, honest talks. She insightfully assisted me in seeing that, much of the time when I help others, I am doing so in large part because of what Denise instilled in me. Who I am today is a direct reflection of the person Denise wanted me to be and the one she helped me to become. By being who I am and continuing to help others, I carry on Denise's legacy and pass that on to other people who might not have even known her. Amber is a true inspiration. I only wish I handled myself with the grace and brilliance she does.

Every night before I go to bed and every morning when I wake up, the first and last thing I do is take off and put on my necklace. Denise's wedding ring continues to hang around my neck. She will always be a part of me and hopefully, as time goes on, I will make her proud. I hope that in some small way I can carry on her legacy for years to come.

Chapter 21

Looking Back and Looking Forward

As I continue to look back on both the five years with Denise and the five years without her, my feelings both lift my spirits and bring me sorrow. I absolutely loved my five years with Denise. I equally hated my five years without her. I'm in a much better place than I was, but that doesn't mean I was wrong to despise the world a couple of years ago. When you have reached the heights of joy only to fall in a single unimaginable instant into the depths of pain, the suffering that follows elicits all sorts of reactions that were previously inconceivable.

On the five-year anniversary of Denise's passing, my wonderful running relay team finished our 200 miles. Being at the beach with my friends was a gift. No one said anything. I believe they probably knew of the date, but we wanted to stay in the moment. That was the right way to enjoy the end of the race.

As the relay ended, I was able to catch up with the sister of my friend Melissa Royer, our wonderful friend who bought my house. At the finish line, Melissa's sister approached me and, realizing it was the anniversary of Denise's passing, wanted to give me some well wishes. Having her acknowledge that day and what it meant while remaining in the moment and in the sunshine meant a lot to me. I recalled that first year when I struggled to enjoy the good moments. Here I stood after five years, enjoying the sunlight on my skin and the time with friends.

Once we all drove home and I got back into my apartment, I did a load of laundry, took a much needed shower, and put on Denise's video. For so long, transitioning from good moments back into my empty house was really hard. Here I was coming from a 30+ hour trip with a bunch of friends and a whole lot of laughs back into my apartment alone. And I was watching all those pictures of Denise move past in the video, something that brought a huge emotional release during those first years. This time, I viewed those snapshots, even the one taken during her first trimester, from a more healed place. While a part of me still thinks I should be sobbing on the floor in a fetal position, I know that's not what Denise wants from me.

As I watched the video, I felt the sadness again but not necessarily for me. I felt it for Denise, for all the years she dreamed of holding and raising babies, for the life she didn't get to live. I probably spent too much of the last few years being sad for me and maybe not enough time feeling sorrow for the woman I loved. I just watched the video and thought about how Denise didn't deserve any of what happened to her. Like me, she believed in the goodness of the world. Maybe we shouldn't have. Had I been aware of what I know now, I would have acted differently. But we didn't know. We just felt if we were good people, we would be rewarded with the life we desired. It was easy to buy into that narrative when we finally found out we were having twins, a boy and a girl, selling our old house, and buying our new one. We climbed to such heights and never expected the fall that was to come.

I'll probably feel the anger over this tragedy to some degree for the rest of my life. But I'm actually functional. I can talk openly about my faults and share my experiences. I attribute that progression in part to the fact that I never pretended this wasn't the worst thing I could ever imagine happening. I leaned into the grief and recognized this loss as the tragedy it truly was.

I regret probably ruining relationships because of how deeply into the grief I dove, but maybe I had to sacrifice some friendships to get to where I am now. I definitely made my life harder so that maybe the next chapter of my life would be easier. To all those people I may have hurt along the way, I'm sorry. This was the only way I knew how to deal with the pain.

I always said I wanted to read the story of the guy who didn't make it, the person who knew the pain I was in, and I still believe that. When you are so mad at the world, the only thing you care about is knowing that you're not alone and that other people have those same thoughts and feelings.

I found outlets for support and ways to deal with the depression I developed then and continue to experience. My mental illness isn't as strong as it was a couple of years ago, and my therapist and I always have fun conversations when I broach the subject. We both acknowledge that I have what she calls an "adjustment disorder." She isn't wrong, but we both know it falls under the umbrella that is mental illness. My therapist is absolutely correct that my mental illness was dropped into my lap. I didn't do anything to make this happen. I had everything one day and the next my world was ripped away from me. That type of tragedy can happen to anyone.

Had I pretended that I wasn't experiencing a deep depression, I would have failed to put my support systems into place when I did and might not be here right now. Even if I had managed to live, I probably would have been unable to talk openly about this devastating loss and its aftermath, and that would have denied a part of Denise's legacy. I was willing to walk headlong into the deepest chasm and eventually climb out the other side. I'm thankful I took the long road, that I played the long game.

When people see me these days, I'm different from the person I was in recent years. Because I now appear pleasantly upbeat most of the time, others think I turned out okay. This assessment is both right and wrong. Yes, I've navigated the worst years and have worked hard to get where I am. I'm proud of that. However, it's not like my life is wonderful.

I'm a 39-year-old special education teacher who lives in a one bedroom, one bathroom apartment, and I am still alone. Those are the facts. On a scale of one to ten, my life on the surface is around a five. The difference is that I can view that five like an eight or nine because I was at zero to two on that scale for years. I hated the person I was during those first two years, and I didn't enjoy who I was for a long time after that. I've been able to make progress, but my life still is not at the level I would want it to be.

I could say that my life sucked, which it did, but you could also make the argument that my life had "growth potential." That means I had the ability to see better times ahead. Of course, I had nowhere to go but up.

When I was thinking of a title of my first book, I would put ideas into my phone. Some of the potential titles included *The 23rd of Every Month*, *I Don't Want This Life*, and even *When It Is All...* (poop emoji). I wanted words to express the darkness that I was feeling. Over time, as I watched more sports events on TV, I noticed people using the statement, "Dreams really do come true." I realized no one ever uses the opposite of that sentiment. We don't hear basketball or football players say, "I want to thank God for giving our team the strength to get blown out and humiliated today."

I know that we always want to stay positive, but refusing to acknowledge the negative side doesn't properly prepare people for the realities of life. I am as much at fault as anyone in this regard. My dad has always been positive, and I couldn't be more inspired by him. I want to be the type of person who brings out the best in people. But when this tragedy occurred, I knew I brought out the worst in those around me. I can't tell you how odd I felt being around families and realizing that as soon as I left they would look at each other and feel really thankful my circumstances hadn't happened to them.

When we only talk about the good in the world, we are not being truly honest. I hated that I saw so much of the darkness in the world, but I also am glad I now can have conversations with people who are down on their luck and are fighting addictions because I know how close I came to all of that.

This was truly a nightmare, one that has stayed with me for the last five years. Being able to handle it better does nothing to alter the fact that it was a nightmare. I am not as raw as I was a couple of years ago, but that doesn't mean my feelings then weren't true and honest. Grieving is a process that goes up and down and circles around. I still remember that first Christmas in the shower when I understood why suicide rates go up at that time of year. I never want to forget that feeling. I can be upbeat now that I have progressed so far from that moment, and that experience is why I can feel for those who are struggling.

Every day, I wake up and put on the necklace with Denise's ring. Every night I place it on the nightstand. It is a symbol of our love and that she is still a part of me. I know she is watching over me, and someday I will get to join her. Until that day, I hope she continues to watch over me and hear my prayers. I still ask God to care for and protect my friends and family, but I hope Denise still stands with me through my good and bad decisions, my triumphs and my defeats.

There are people who don't acknowledge me these days and some I feel comfortable saying plain don't like me. That's fine. I am who I am and I'm proud of the man I've become. If they couldn't even acknowledge the pain I was in or help me through it, they probably could not have lived my life. For those who were there for me during the worst days, I won't forget it. For those who weren't, I'm just thankful you didn't have to face this kind of tragedy.

One of the most important aspects of my life going forward deals with Denise's family. We were thrust into the fire and allowed it to scorch us and burn down our relationship perhaps more than we should have. I take responsibility for my part in how that unfolded. Many of the books I read discussed how families often don't survive such devastating losses. The reality was the connection that brought us together was gone and she would never come back. We all were pushed to the limits, and some might say we failed while others might say we passed.

Everything comes down to one simple question: Do we love Denise? I can firmly say that we all love her, which is why we will be okay. We may not be together on holidays and may live very different lives, but that truth remains no matter what. I love them and I'm sure they love me because we all loved Denise. I don't expect them to be fully present in my life, but her family will always be a part of my journey.

I know that Denise would love to see me get remarried and that her family would too. I don't know what the future holds. Friends of mine tell me that my idea of a mail-order bride isn't the best option during this time (thanks, pandemic), but I believe I can love someone again. I think I can be in a healthy relationship. I have opened myself to that possibility, and we will see where it goes. I still haven't gone on a date, but I need to be patient, which is something I haven't been great at these last few years.

I know I will always feel for those who are experiencing grief on any level. A little part of me will always compare my experience to those of others. I have to be honest with myself about that. Nonetheless, I hope that others know I'm here for them whatever their circumstances. Because people weren't always there for me, and I know what that feels like, it's even more important for me to support others who walk this path of grief.

I always wanted to hear people's reasons for not reaching out to me as much as I expected them to. However, most were probably too concerned about what to say and feared being honest with me, so they just turned away. This is why I lived on an island during much of my journey through grief. I wish people could simply have been honest with me instead of sheltering me from the possibility of hurt feelings, which actually did more damage to my psyche.

I can't imagine I will ever live through anything like this again, although I would be foolish to think that bad things weren't in store for me. It's going to be incredibly difficult when my parents pass away. They have done so much to help me heal and navigate my grief. The nightmare of Denise's death and the aftermath of such a loss for her parents, sister, and family was devastating beyond belief, but my own parents' journey through this horror was far from easy. They had to watch their only son fall apart. At any moment, on the other side of the ringing phone, they had no idea what they were going to hear and what kind of shape I was going to be in.

I received a lot of help and support over the years. It's definitely easier for people to talk to me now than it was, but it's also important to look back and think about what helped me get to where I am. I did this in the first book as a way of gauging my progress and wanted to revisit the idea.

Here are the top three internal factors that helped me get through:

This first one is easy: Denise. She is the reason I am who I am. A large part of me still lives and carries on because I want to better tell her story and to do her life justice. She deserves so much more than my inadequate words and unique writing style, but she is the reason I made it this far. I didn't want this tragedy to wipe out her memory.

Next is and forever will be the hero we all need and the hero we all want. No, I'm not talking about Iron Man or whatever Marvel character is big when you read this. My superhero is my father. I can't begin to describe how impactful he is to me. He is everything I aspire to be. Even after all of this, I hope I can smile the way he does and manage to say yes even when I want to say no. As I get older, I hope to become just like him.

Finally, the biggest internal factor was my self-discipline. I have always lived an extremely structured life. But I had to take that discipline to a new level and make sure I found all the resources, content, and therapy to travel the road to healing.

In addition to these internal factors, there are a few external factors that need to be identified. One of my most powerful reasons for making it this far has to do with my work. The teachers, administrators, and, most importantly, those kids at school gave me a safe haven, a bridge to the world, and smiles when there wasn't much to smile about. My strength as a teacher relies on the relationships I build with kids, and those relationships provided the only real, day-to-day moments of joy in a world that seemed so cruel I often didn't want to be a part of it.

Another factor that saw me through these times was my desire to stay active. Being able to go to the gym, jump on the elliptical, or lace up my shoes and run or walk was instrumental on this uphill climb through uncharted territory. Exercise has been so beneficial in regard to fighting of all the lonely hours and the sleep deprivation, and it helped me to develop positive friendships.

Finally, my sleep medication has been vital to my recovery. Getting those few hours of sleep during the enormous depression I experienced was so important. I know that our addiction to medication is troublesome to say the least, but without that medication my brain wouldn't shut down on its own at the time. I was thankful that as I got better I weaned myself off the meds, but they helped me get much-needed rest during those desperate times.

I believe I will join Denise and get to hold our babies when this life is over. I can say how much better I'm doing, which is true, but the reality is I still have barriers to cross. The biggest one probably relates to the loss of our twins.

There is a real possibility that I might never have children. I see kids everywhere, and it's a very real worry I have. I think if that happens and I am married to someone I love, I will be able to accept this disappointment. I know I will be sad if I never get to have children of my own, but, as I learned after Denise died, I can't isolate myself because of the pain. I hold on to hope but don't want to allow the world to crush those hopes again.

I still struggle with checking and double checking things. I'm the guy staring at my car, making sure it's locked, and touching the top of each window to be certain they are shut all the way. Luckily, my obsessiveness doesn't interfere with my day-to-day responsibilities, but I still find it embarrassing. As much as I try to do better, this is one area I haven't made the type of progress I hope for. I have done better with the stove because my new apartment has a warm surface light, so thankfully I don't have to check each knob before going to bed. I am going to continue to deal with my mental health.

I realize the past still impacts me in countless ways, especially every time I walk into a doctor's office. I know my own doctor loves me and wants the best for me, but I can't be certain about the person who signs her checks. My experience with the business side of the medical community after Denise died revealed their tendency to suppress an honest, heartfelt response and make decisions with their wallets instead of their hearts. I probably will always have that inner demon telling me that there are people in the medical community that don't care. It will take some time for me to recover from their callous disregard for my grief.

At some point I will buy a new house. After I moved into my new apartment, the real estate market went wild, so I'll stay in the apartment until things settle down. It gives me more time to heal. As disappointing as the housing market shift was, I'm still glad I went full reset on my life.

Just as I have opened myself up to the possibility of dating, I have become ready to buy a house. Although I didn't get it, I put an offer on a home. It was another step forward. I continue to challenge myself and try to be the best version of myself, the one that Denise loved.

Someday, the dating and the second life will hopefully come together. I still have plenty to work on until then. I think a lot about the evolution of my role in Denise's family and still feel disappointed by how things turned out. My big fear was that by losing them, I was losing part of Denise. As time went on, I realized Denise will always be a part of me. Whether I'm close to her family and friends or not, she will always have a place in my heart. Coming to that realization helped settle much of my anxiety regarding the family dynamics.

I still need to work on my jealousy. Before leaving the house after one of my conversations, one of Denise's best friends told me I should worry more about other people, those who also were having a hard time coping with the loss. Sadly, in my grief and anger, I could only see that those people whom I relied on to be there in my mourning, to help me heal from the loss, had remained distant and kept me at arm's length. Under the circumstances, I found it difficult to feel bad for them when they had families and lives that went on as I struggled just to survive.

I realize that Denise didn't belong to me. She belonged to everyone. If people struggled with her loss, that says more about their love for Denise than about their unwillingness to help me.

I need to make sure my jealousy of those leading joyful lives doesn't interfere with the happiness of others. When good things happen to the people who clearly cared, I will continue to feel overjoyed for them. However, I find it challenging to feel that way when it comes to the people who slammed the door on my sorrow and chose not to support me in my time of greatest need. I hope to become more empathetic toward them in the future. It will not be easy, but I know it's what Denise would want, so I will work on forgiveness and acceptance. The world can be loving, gentle, and kind, but it can also be unsympathetic, dark, and cruel. I've experienced both the positive side during our first five years together and the bleakest side of life after Denise died.

I doubt I will ever be a better person than I was the day before Denise died. But maybe I can affect change and perhaps my story can help people. I dislike burdening people with the tragedy of my story and knowing that any unsuspecting person is only three simple questions away from feeling shock and sorrow. At the same time, I want people to know that I made it through, that I did survive, that sometimes the best thing to do is the hardest. I leaned so far into the grief that I thought its flames might consume me. I flew extremely close to the sun, trying to free myself from the pain in the long run, but somehow I didn't get burned. I'm still here. To quote Robert Frost, "I took the road less traveled."

I'm not who I think I could have been, but that was taken from me five years ago. I'm a different me now. I'm comfortable with the man I've become and thankful for how far I've come.

Denise, I love you, I love you, I love you. That part of the story never ends.

Acknowledgments:

I would like to thank all those people who reached out, got into a room with me, and provided much needed support. I will spend the rest of my life expressing my gratitude to you for all the support you gave me. I'm alive in large part because you were there for me.

I would like to give a special thank you to the following people: Mr. Bob, Teshia Utley-McKoy, Jeff Kent, Jared Boyer, Tim Morris, Dirk Wynne, Derek Hurdle, William and Anthony Lucas, Eileen Galligan, Lindsay Vollmin, Meredith Poole, Kayla Williams, Jeannie Simonds, Katie Ring, Emily Quigley, Mary Warren, Jennifer Lanane, Aileen Wala, Jessica Beisler, Ryan Blackwell, Thomas and Melissa Royer, Kevin Butler, the Gardinier family, the McKay family, the Huffman family, and my amazing principal, Danielle Clark, who did such a great job helping me transition back into the classroom and the world.

Also, thank you to the people who greatly helped taking my words from the computer to this book: Jill Eagan, Drew Becker, and Diana Henderson.

Additionally, I would like to thank Roger Nott, Jennifer McKinnon, Jan Hargrove, my widow's group, Amber Belkofer, Walter Harris, Evan Wimpey, Lynwood Sherin, Ben Slocum, Todd Finkbone, Rick Williams, the Kent Family, Tim Obrien, Thirza Whitney, Gail Zadell, the Drury Family, Greg Delbridge, Quinn Novels, Josephine Macon, Lois and Tom Galligan, Rachel Gillespie, Alyssa Burke, Jon Lussier, Suzon Luke, Brenna Harvey and the HSES Office Staff, the Swayney family, the Halsey Family, and Sara Swayney.

I want to acknowledge the University of North Carolina Medical School for giving me a chance to talk about my experiences and for sharing my belief in the power of education. I know it wasn't easy, but you all met, properly vetted me, and believed in me. I will always consider yours a world-class educational institution and medical school.

As always, I offer my deepest gratitude to my loving mother and my hero and inspiration, my father.

I would like to thank Denise for making me the man I am today. I sincerely hope I have made you proud.

About the Author

Levi Moore lives in Raleigh, North Carolina. He has his undergraduate degree and master's degree in Special Education. He has taught elementary Special Education for 16 years. Levi enjoys running, reading, and watching movies and sports. This is his second book. Levi is on Twitter @ LeviMMoore.

www.ingramcontent.com/pod-product-compliance
Lightning Source LLC
Chambersburg PA
CBHW072002110526
44592CB00012B/1175